Natsuki Hokami

While I was drawing, I remembered something: I really like those jelly drinks that you have to shake. There was a vending machine at the high school I went that sold a mango gelatin in the summer, and I bought a ton of them. I suppose those gelatins are probably gone by now.

Natsuki Hokami's first serialized manga, *Hell Warden Higuma*, was published in *Weekly Shonen Jump* in 2018.

Demon Slayer: Kimetsu Academy

VOLUME 2
SHONEN JUMP EDITION

STORY AND ART BY
NATSUKI HOKAMI

Translation / John Werry
Touch-Up Art & Lettering / E.K. Weaver
Design / Yukiko Whitley
Editor / Andrew Kuhre Bartosh

KIMETSU GAKUEN! © 2021 by Koyoharu Gotouge, Natsuki Hokami
All rights reserved.
First published in Japan in 2021 by SHUEISHA Inc., Tokyo.
English translation rights arranged by SHUEISHA Inc.

Printed in the U.S.A.

Published by VIZ Media, LLC
P.O. Box 77010
San Francisco, CA 94107

10 9 8 7 6 5 4 3 2 1
First printing, April 2024

viz.com

DEMON SLAYER KIMETSU ACADEMY

Story and Art by
Natsuki Hokami

Based on Koyoharu Gotouge's
Demon Slayer: Kimetsu no Yaiba

DEMON SLAYER
KIMETSU ACADEMY

CHARACTERS

NEZUKO KAMADO

TARO CLASS
JUNIOR HIGH,
SECOND-YEAR

BAMBOO
SHOOT CLASS
HIGH SCHOOL,
FIRST-YEAR

A serious and polite boy. Wears earrings even though it's against the rules.

Tanjiro's younger sister. Always groggy in the morning.

TANJIRO KAMADO

ZENITSU AGATSUMA

A very moody guy. Part of the disciplinary committee despite Tomioka Sensei's suspicions that his hair is dyed.

A hungry boy who loves tempura. Doesn't bother with books, just his lunch.

BAMBOO
SHOOT CLASS
HIGH SCHOOL,
FIRST-YEAR

INOSUKE HASHIBIRA

BAMBOO
SHOOT CLASS
HIGH SCHOOL,
FIRST-YEAR

CONTENTS

2 The Kimetsu Academy Night Tour

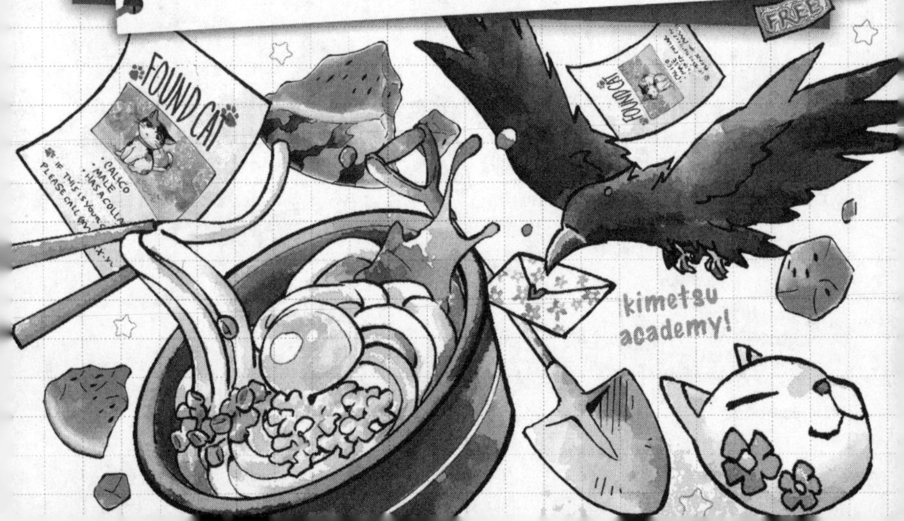

FOUND CAT
kimetsu academy!

CHAPTER 6: CATNIP FOR KITTIES, KITTIES FOR HIMEJIMA

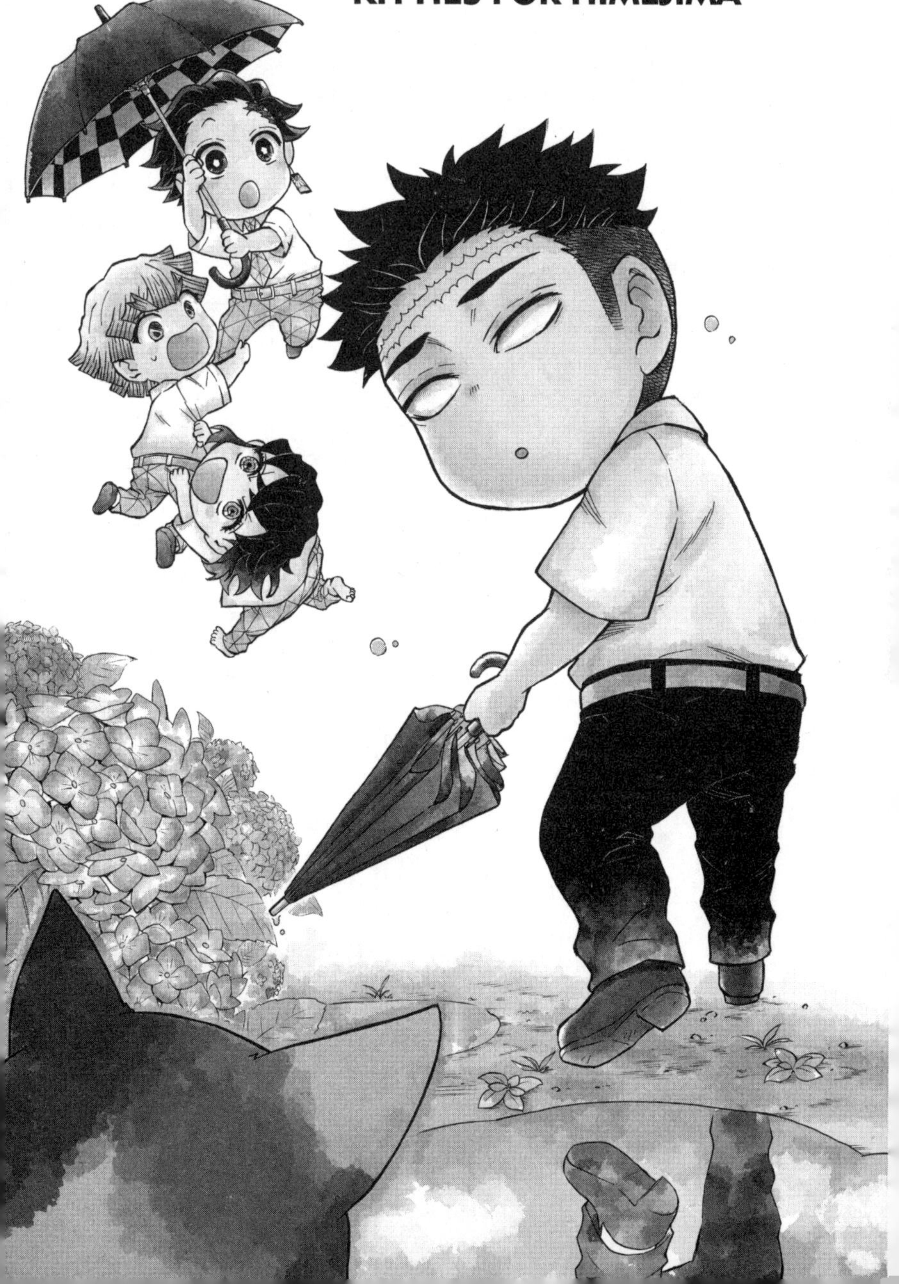

It has a collar.

I THINK IT'S LOST.

IT'S BEEN WANDERING AROUND THE CAMPUS.

I FOUND THIS CAT THE OTHER DAY.

KRNCH KRNCH

AND IT IS SO...

... CUTE!

I LOVE EVERYTHING ABOUT CATS...

...FROM THE WAY THEY LOOK TO HOW THEY BEHAVE.

JUST PETTING ONE IS ENOUGH TO GIVE ME ENERGY BACK.

...OR FEEDING IT ON SCHOOL GROUNDS, BUT...

PURR PURR

I KNOW I SHOULDN'T BE CARING FOR IT IN SECRET...

SIGH

THIS IS JUST UNTIL YOUR OWNER FINDS YOU!

BESIDES, IT'S NOT LIKE ANY STUDENTS WILL FIND ME OUT HERE!

PSS PSS

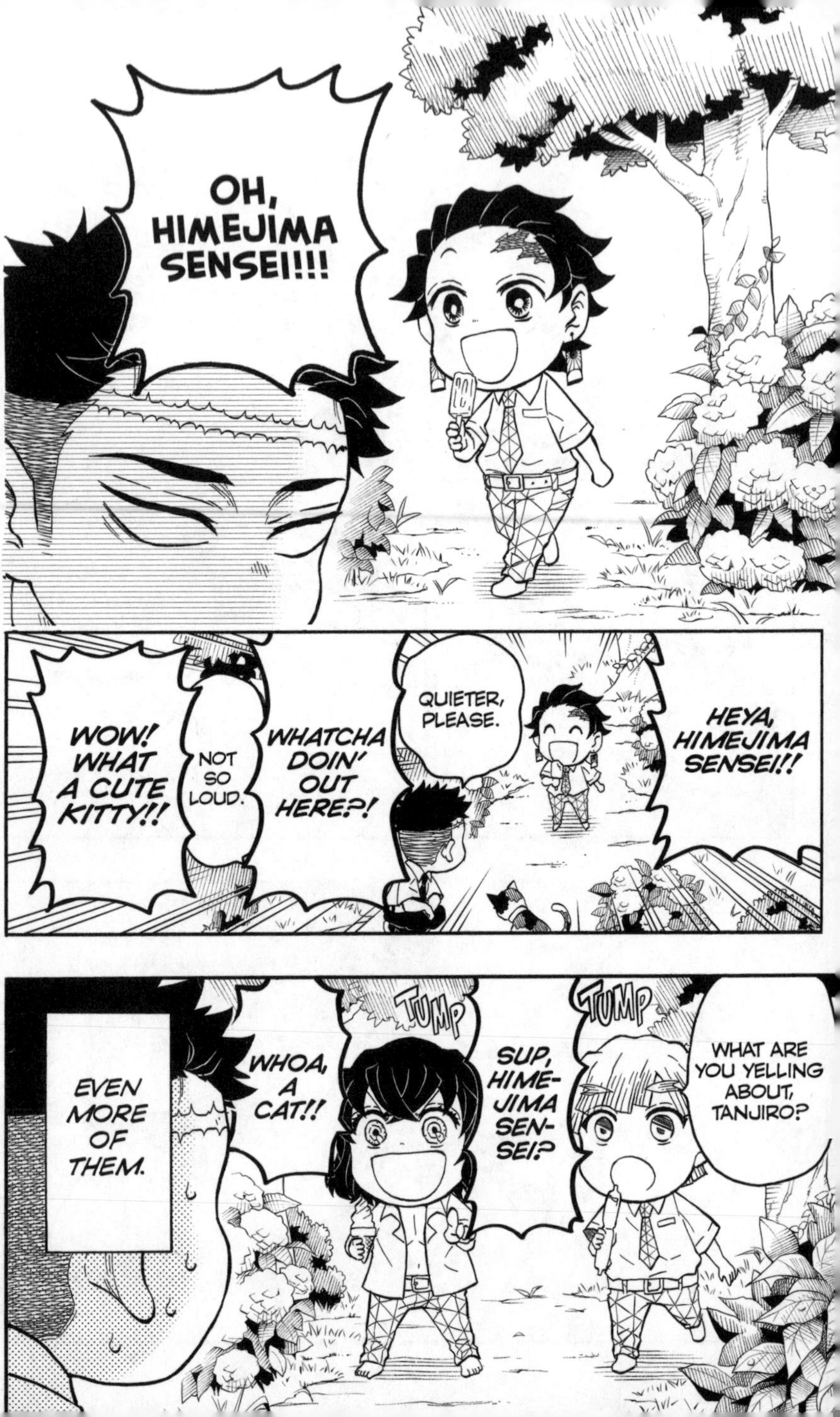
OH, HIMEJIMA SENSEI!!!
HEYA, HIMEJIMA SENSEI!!
QUIETER, PLEASE.
WHATCHA DOIN' OUT HERE?!
NOT SO LOUD.
WOW! WHAT A CUTE KITTY!!
WHAT ARE YOU YELLING ABOUT, TANJIRO?
TUMP
SUP, HIME-JIMA SEN-SEI?
TUMP
WHOA, A CAT!!
EVEN MORE OF THEM.

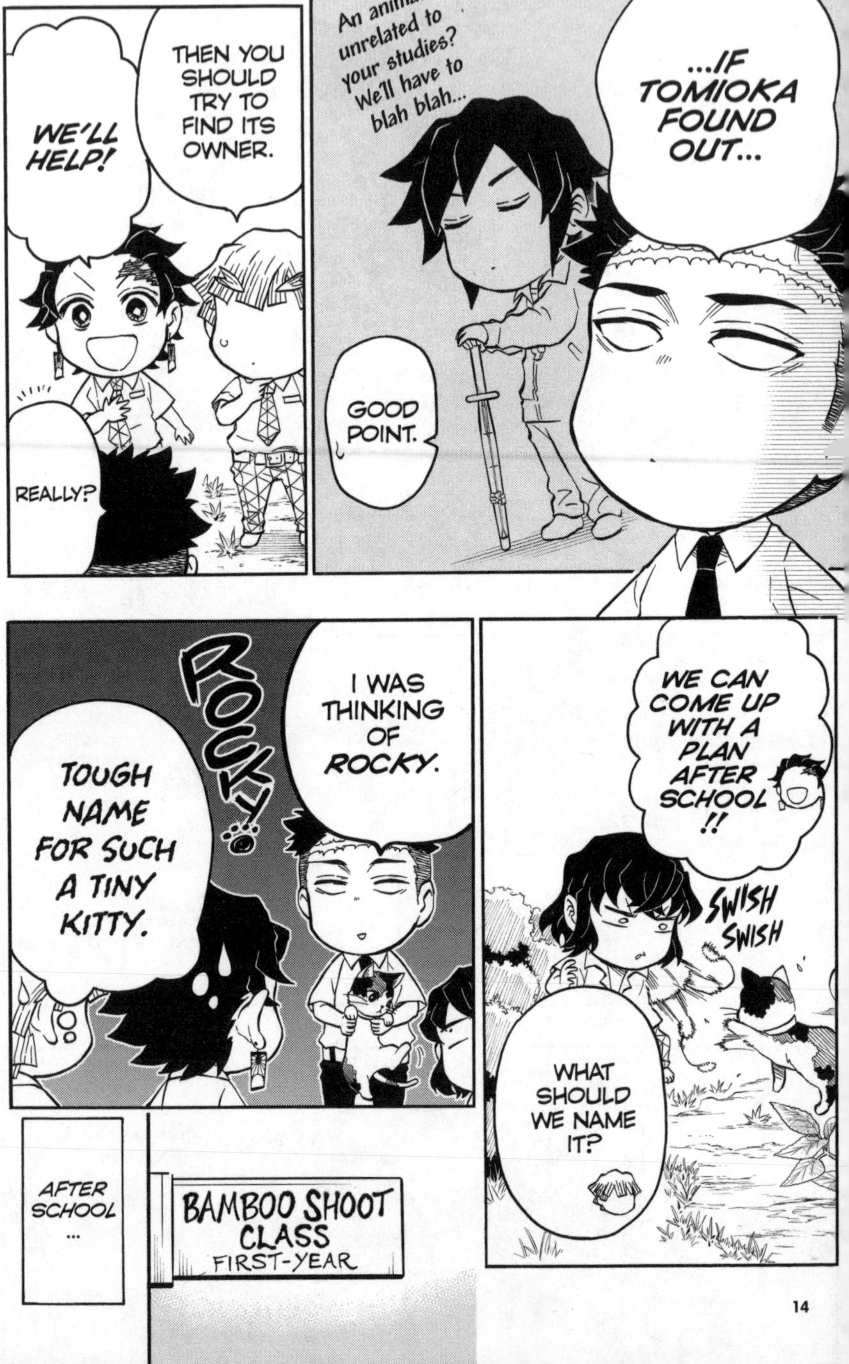
...IF TOMIOKA FOUND OUT...
An animal unrelated to your studies? We'll have to blah blah...
GOOD POINT.
THEN YOU SHOULD TRY TO FIND ITS OWNER.
WE'LL HELP!
REALLY?
WE CAN COME UP WITH A PLAN AFTER SCHOOL!!
SWISH SWISH
WHAT SHOULD WE NAME IT?
I WAS THINKING OF ROCKY.
ROCKY!
TOUGH NAME FOR SUCH A TINY KITTY.
BAMBOO SHOOT CLASS FIRST-YEAR
AFTER SCHOOL ...

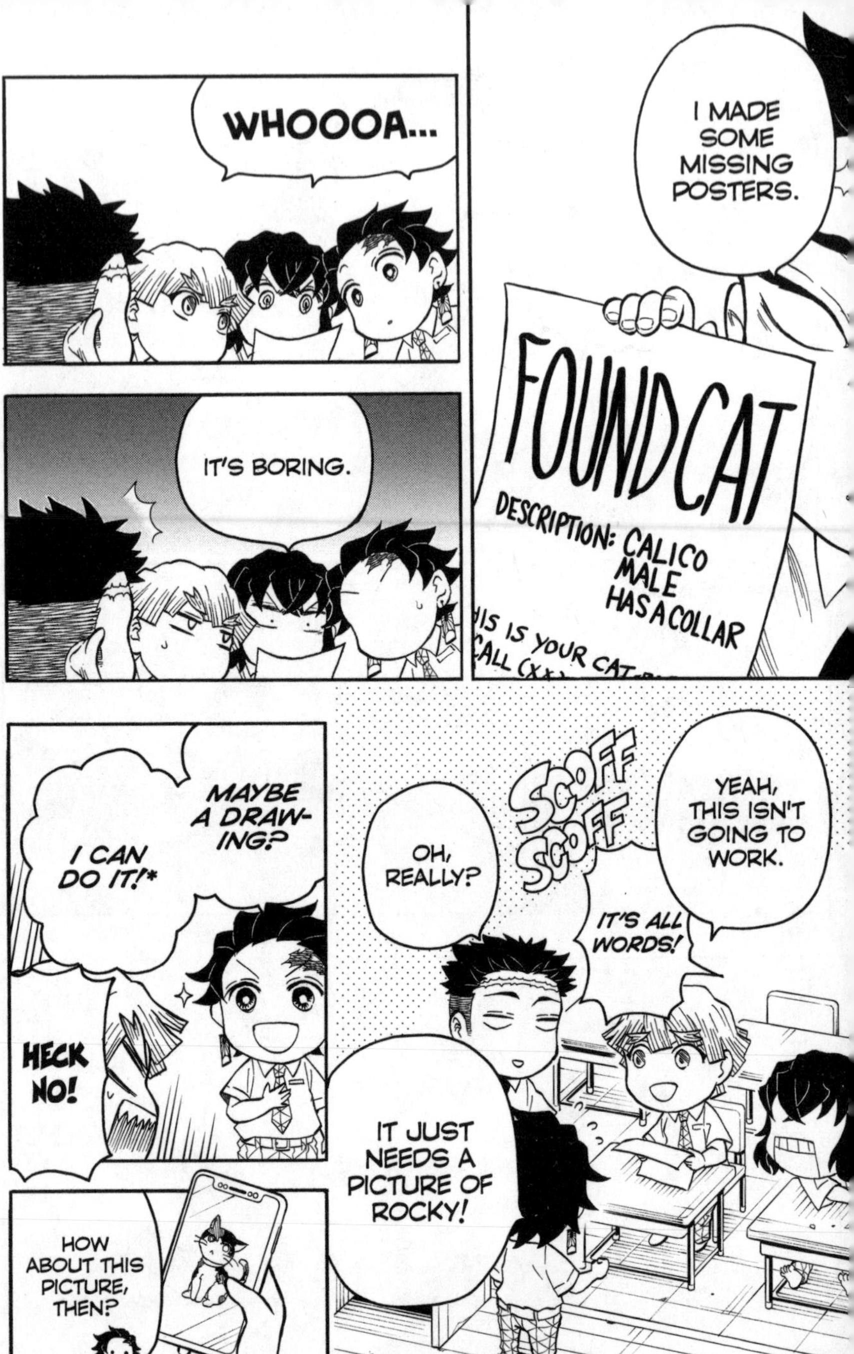
I MADE SOME MISSING POSTERS.
FOUND CAT
DESCRIPTION: CALICO MALE HAS A COLLAR
WHOOOA...
IT'S BORING.
YEAH, THIS ISN'T GOING TO WORK.
IT'S ALL WORDS!
SCOFF SCOFF
OH, REALLY?
IT JUST NEEDS A PICTURE OF ROCKY!
MAYBE A DRAW-ING?
I CAN DO IT!*
HECK NO!
HOW ABOUT THIS PICTURE, THEN?

*CHECK VOLUME 1 TO SEE TANJIRO'S ARTISTIC "SKILLS."

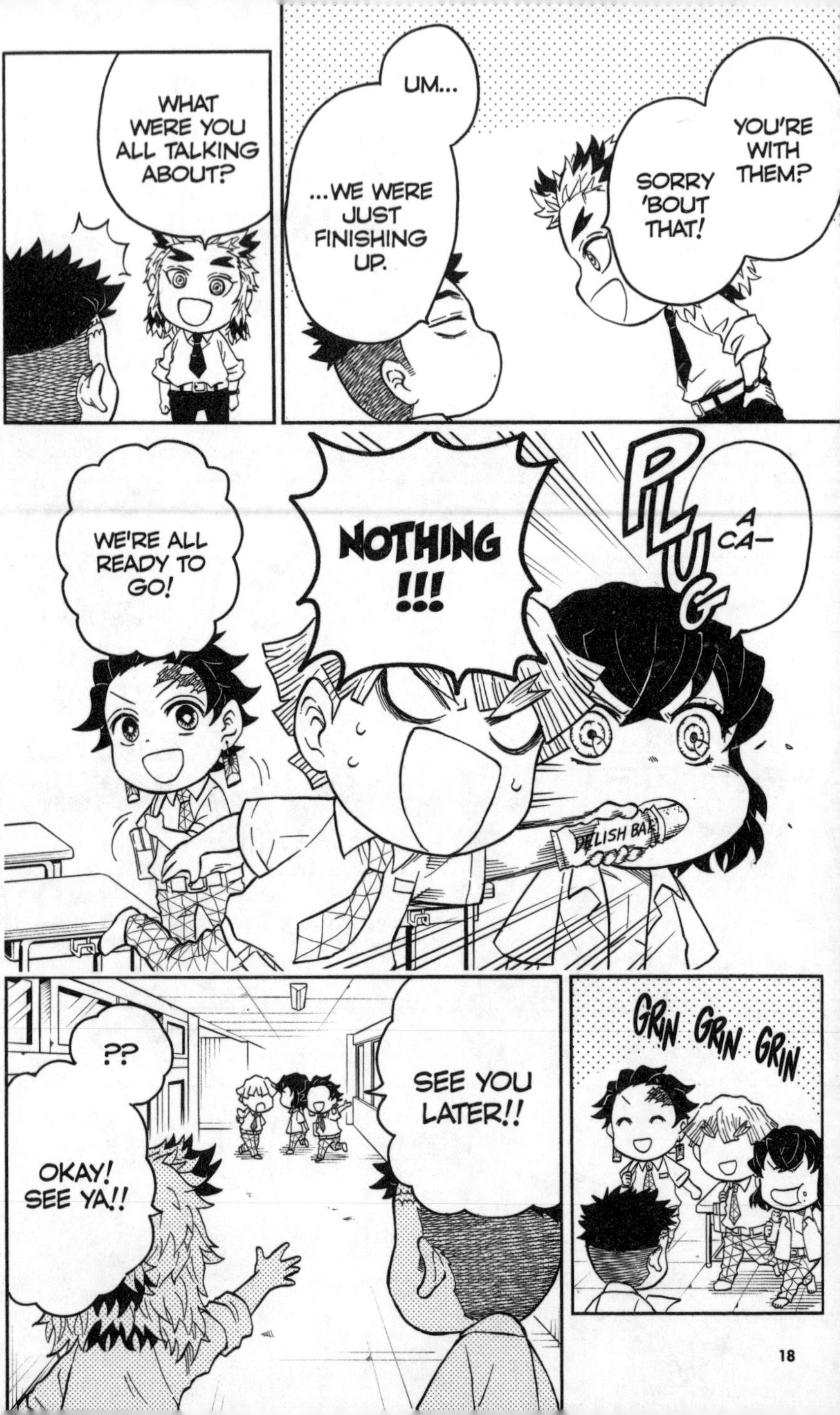
YOU'RE WITH THEM?
SORRY 'BOUT THAT!
UM...
...WE WERE JUST FINISHING UP.
WHAT WERE YOU ALL TALKING ABOUT?
A CA—
PLUG
NOTHING!!!
WE'RE ALL READY TO GO!
GRIN GRIN GRIN
SEE YOU LATER!!
??
OKAY! SEE YA!!

THE THREE OF YOU AREN'T SECRETLY KEEPING THIS CAT ON SCHOOL GROUNDS, ARE YOU?

I SAW KAMADO AND HASHIBIRA...

...PUTTING UP THE SAME NOTICE.

BULLS-EYE

GIYU TOMIOKA
P.E. TEACHER

ZEEEE-NITSUUU!!

I'D NEVER DO SOMETHING LIKE THAT! BUT ONE OF THOSE TWO MIGHT!

W-WHAT? NO! OF COURSE NOT!

I TOTALLY SOLD THEM OUT...

...BUT I'M SURE THEY'LL BE FINE.

PROBABLY.

PHEW

SKF

OH?

THEN I'LL ASK THEM.

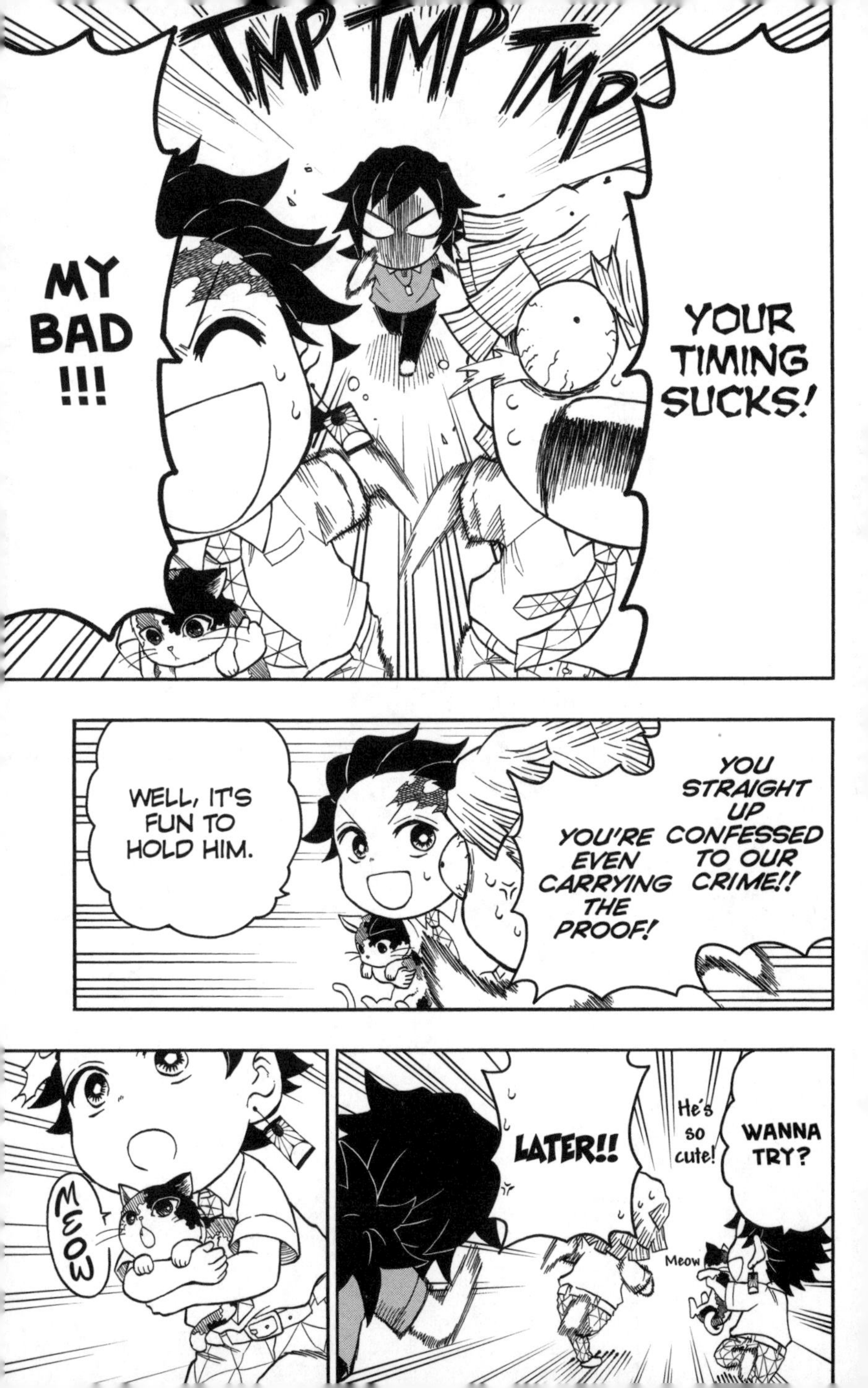
TMP TMP TMP TMP
YOUR TIMING SUCKS!
MY BAD!!!
YOU STRAIGHT UP CONFESSED TO OUR CRIME!!
YOU'RE EVEN CARRYING THE PROOF!
WELL, IT'S FUN TO HOLD HIM.
WANNA TRY?
He's so cute!
LATER!!
Meow
MEOW

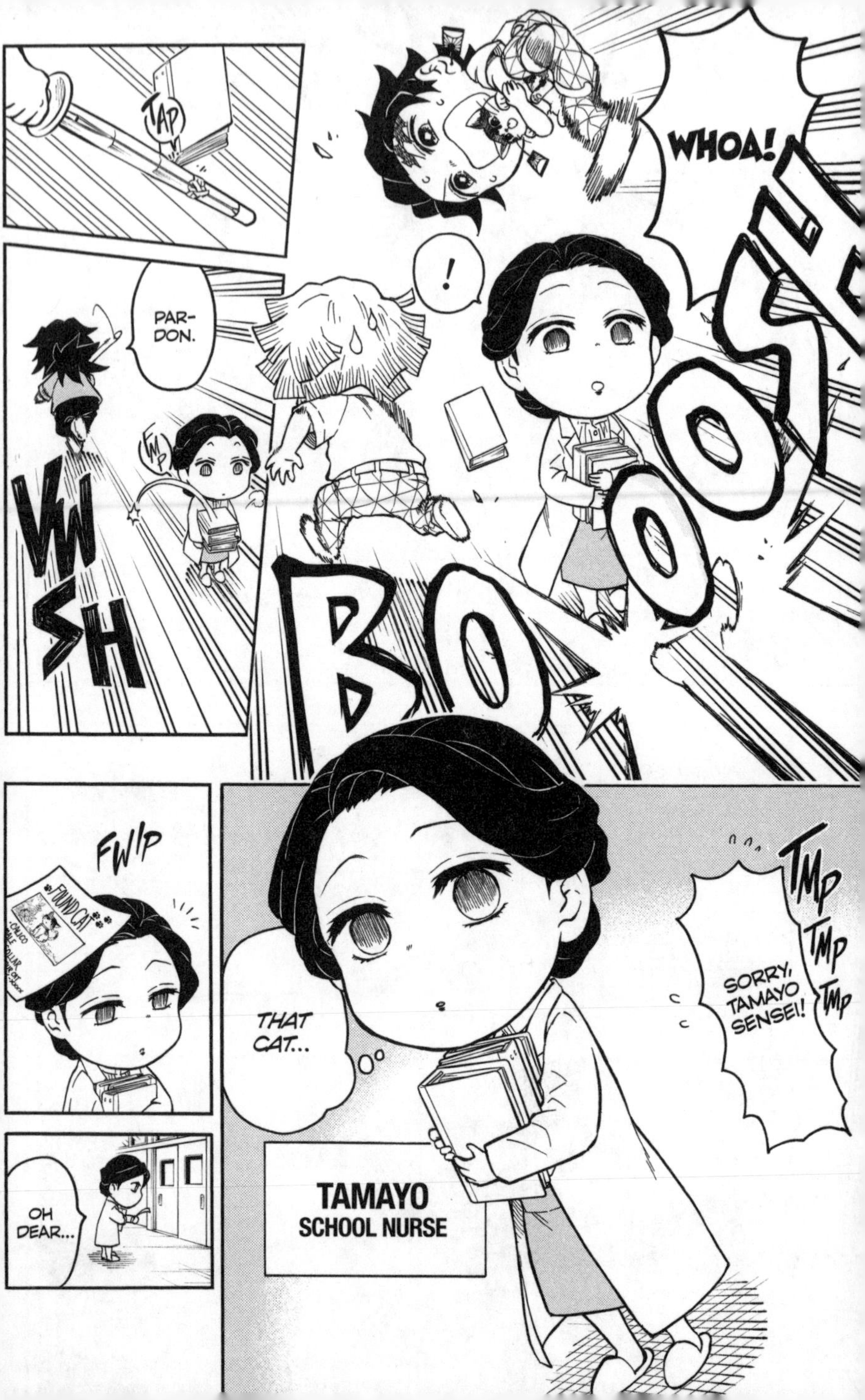
WHOA!
!
BOOOSH
TAP
PAR-DON.
FMP
WHSH
TMP TMP TMP
SORRY, TAMAYO SENSEI!
THAT CAT...
TAMAYO
SCHOOL NURSE
FWIP
FOUND CAT
OH DEAR...

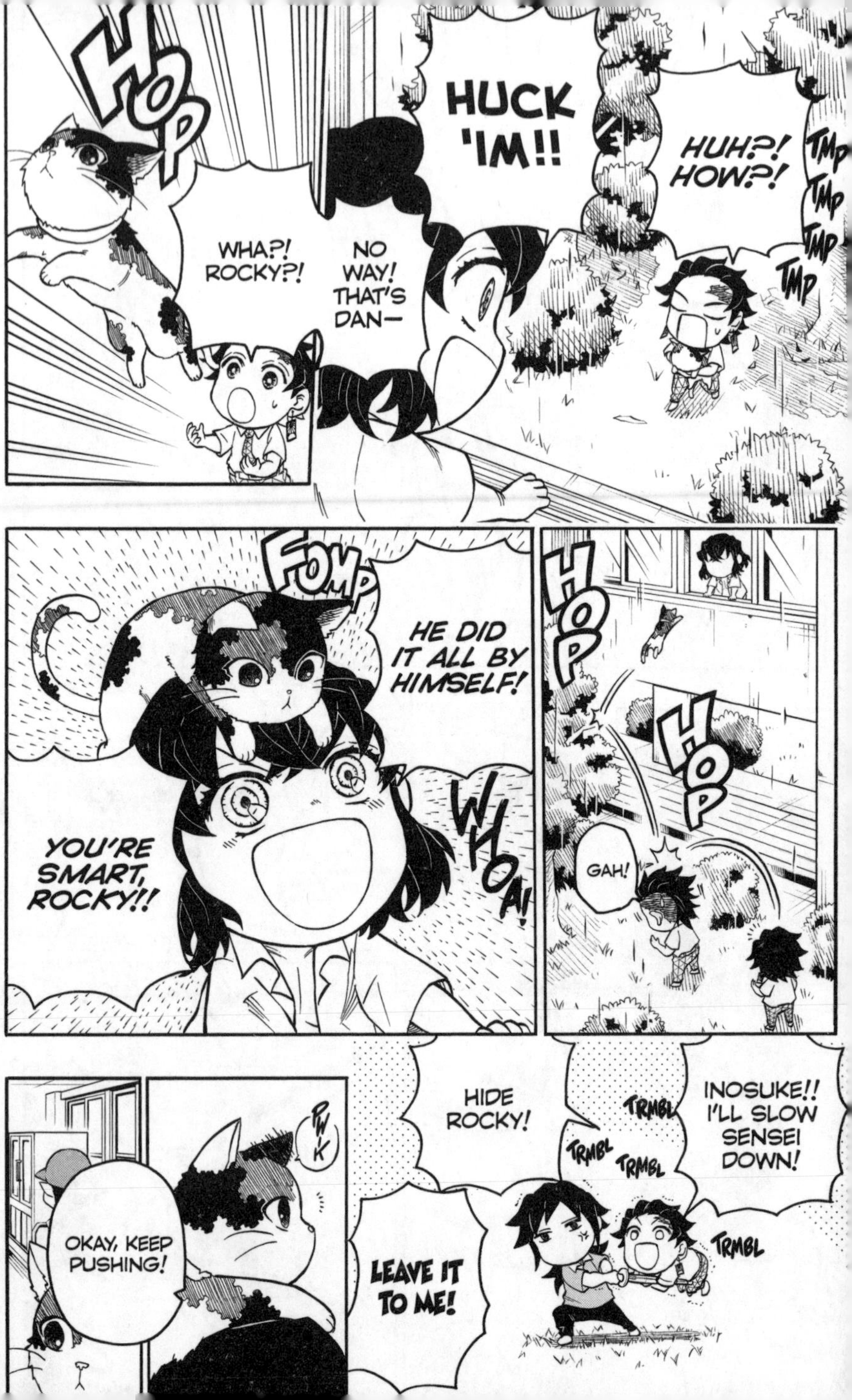
TMP TMP TMP TMP
HUH?! HOW?!
HUCK 'IM!!
NO WAY! THAT'S DAN—
WHA?! ROCKY?!
HOP
HOP
HOP
GAH!
FOMP
HE DID IT ALL BY HIMSELF!
WHOA!
YOU'RE SMART, ROCKY!!
INOSUKE!! I'LL SLOW SENSEI DOWN!
TRMBL TRMBL TRMBL TRMBL
HIDE ROCKY!
LEAVE IT TO ME!
PWK
OKAY, KEEP PUSHING!

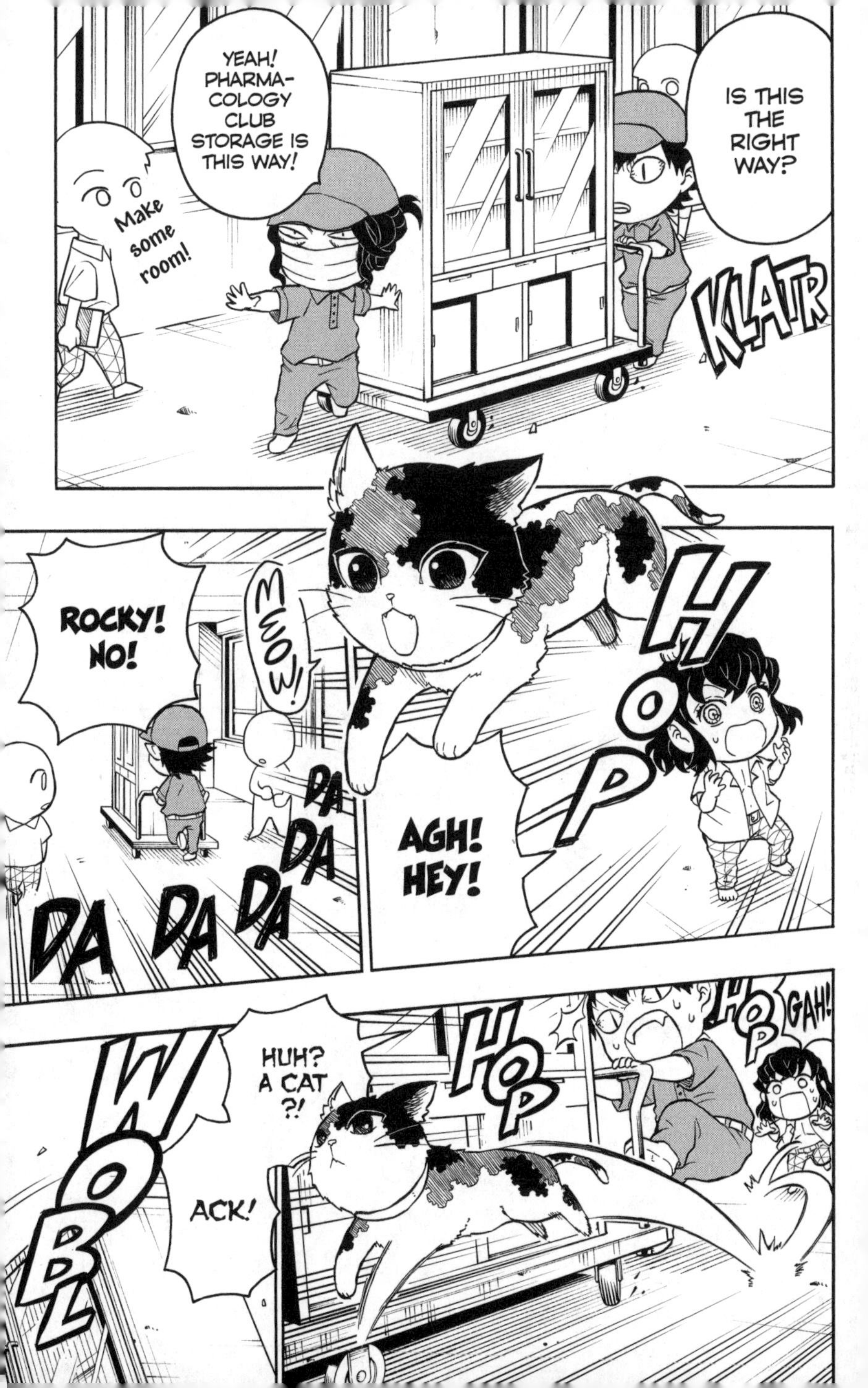
IS THIS THE RIGHT WAY?
YEAH! PHARMA-COLOGY CLUB STORAGE IS THIS WAY!
Make some room!
KLATR
HOP
MEOW!
AGH! HEY!
ROCKY! NO!
DA DA DA DA DA
GAH!
HOP
HOP
HUH? A CAT ?!
ACK!
WOBL

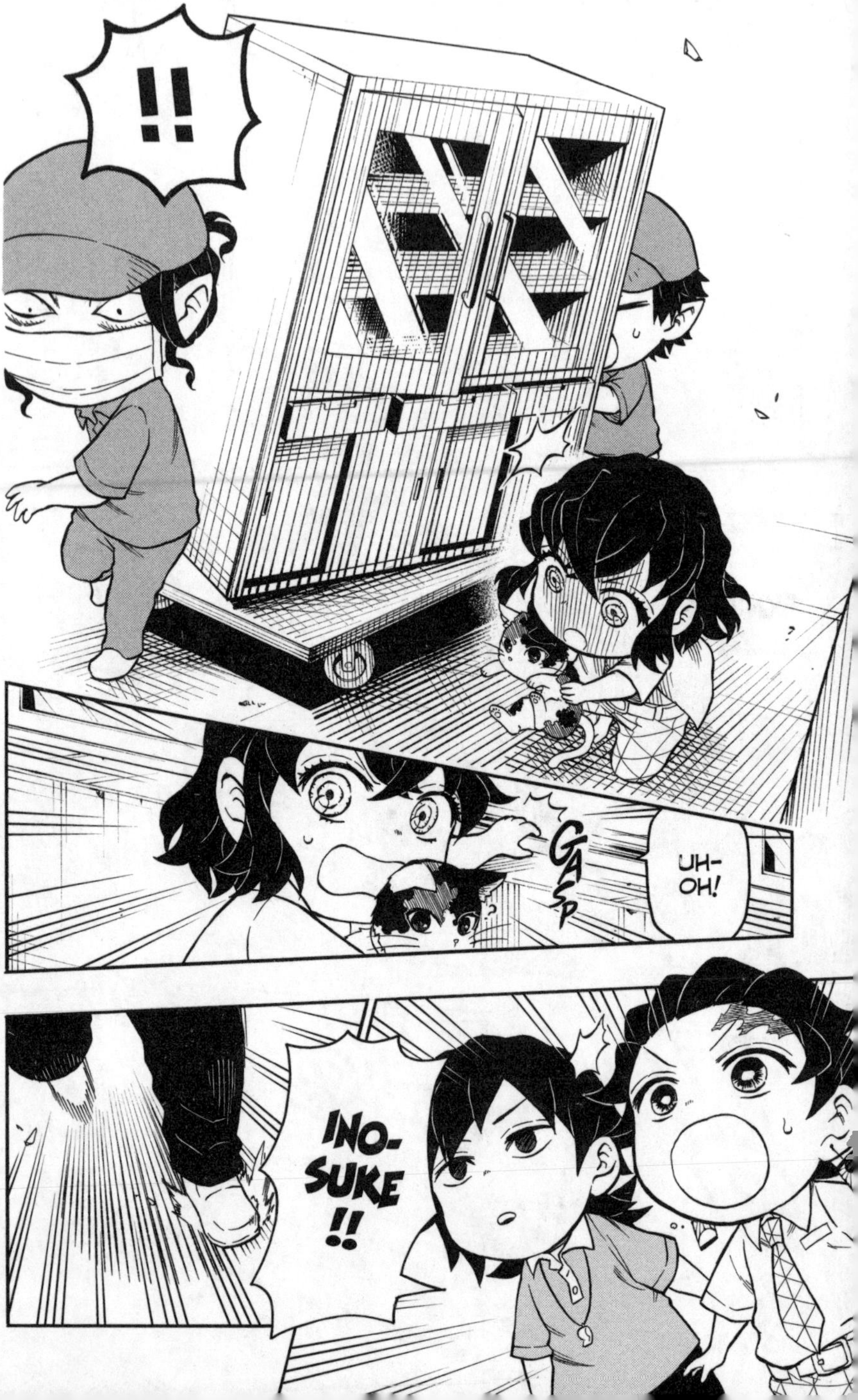
!!
UH-OH!
GASP
INO-SUKE!!

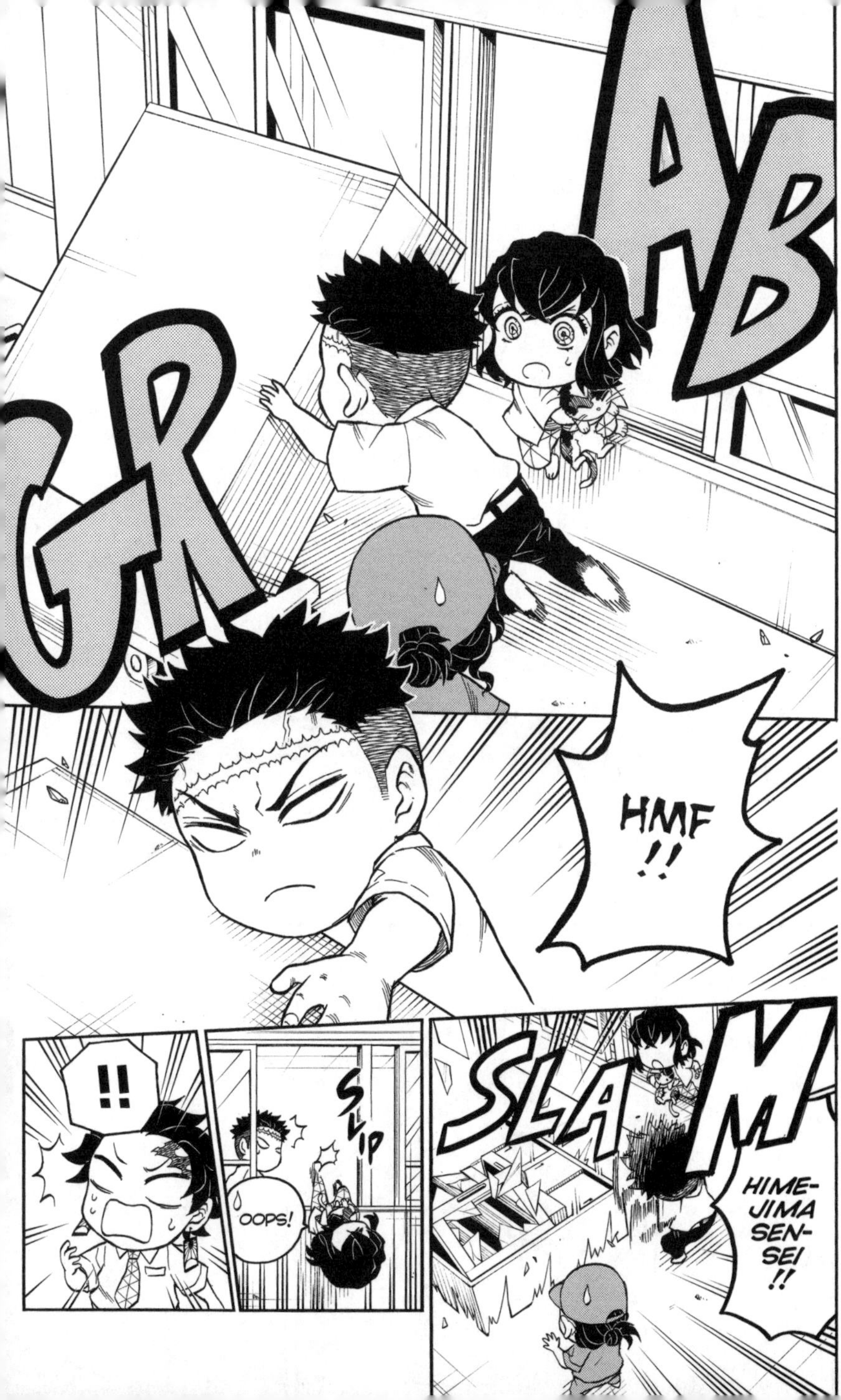
AB
GR
HMF !!
SLAM
HIMEJIMA SENSEI!!
SLIP
OOPS!
!!

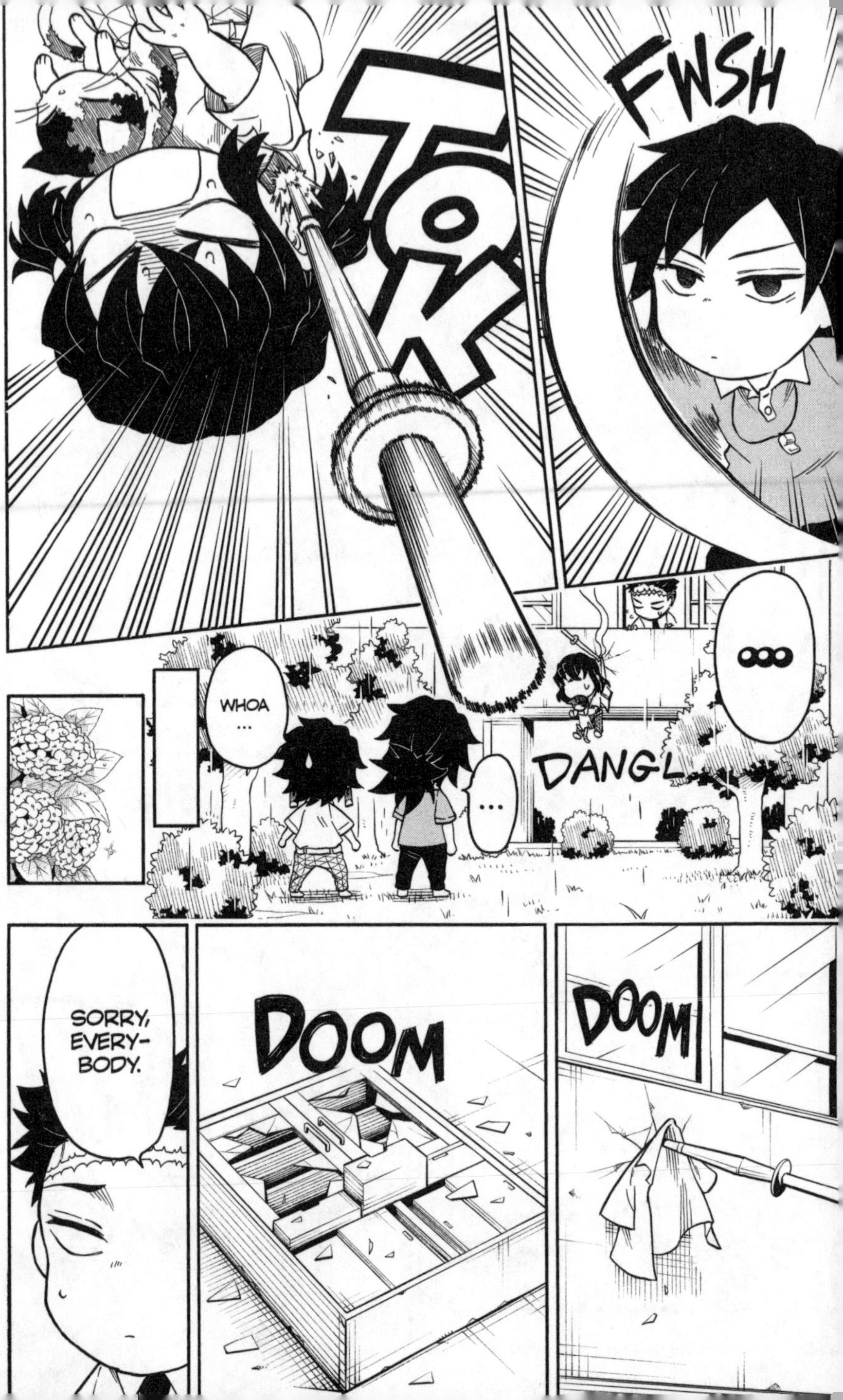
FWSH
TOK
...
DANGL
...
WHOA ...
DOOM
DOOM
SORRY, EVERY-BODY.

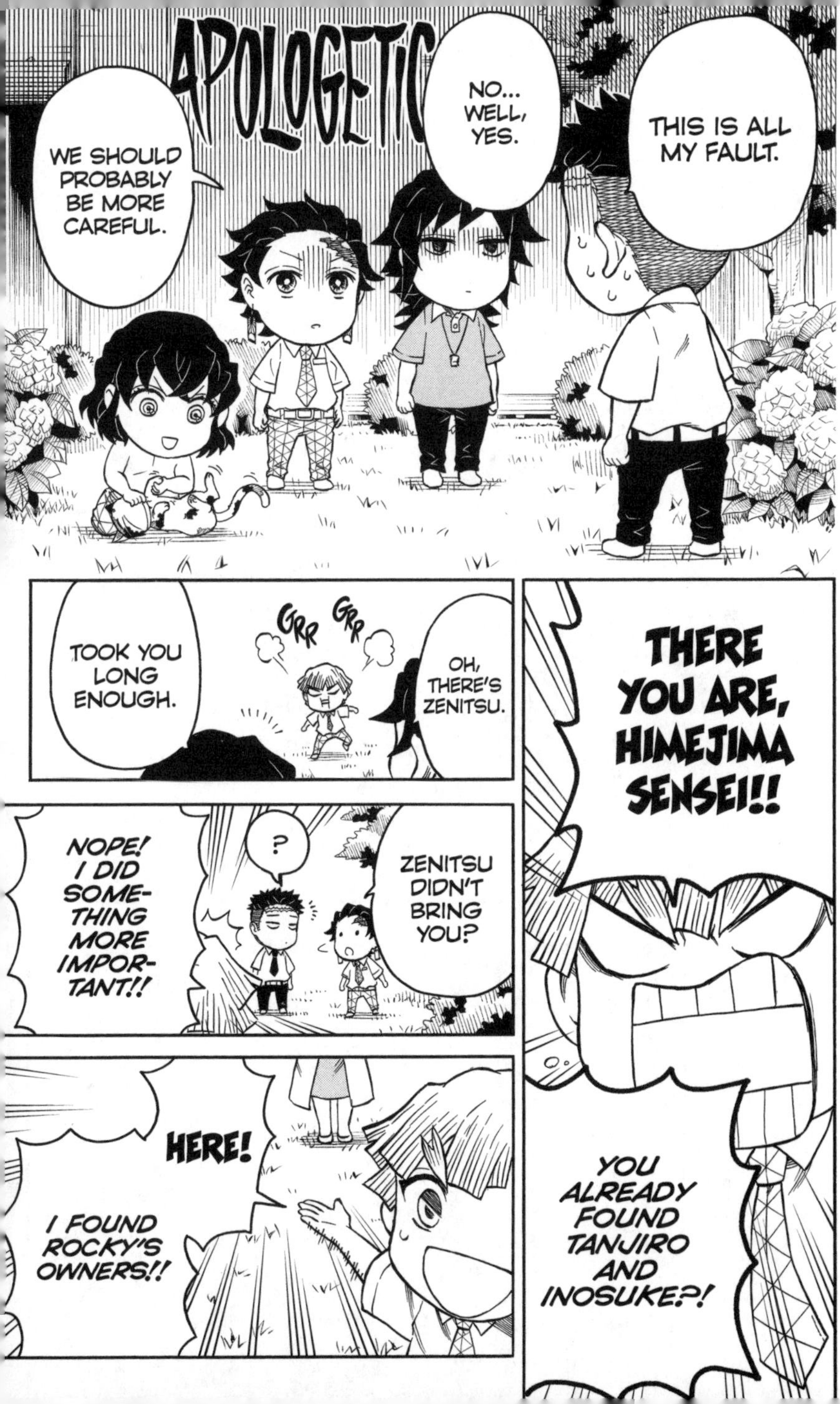
THIS IS ALL MY FAULT.
NO... WELL, YES.
APOLOGETIC
WE SHOULD PROBABLY BE MORE CAREFUL.
THERE YOU ARE, HIMEJIMA SENSEI!!
YOU ALREADY FOUND TANJIRO AND INOSUKE?!
OH, THERE'S ZENITSU.
GRR GRR
TOOK YOU LONG ENOUGH.
ZENITSU DIDN'T BRING YOU?
?
NOPE! I DID SOME-THING MORE IMPOR-TANT!!
HERE!
I FOUND ROCKY'S OWNERS!!

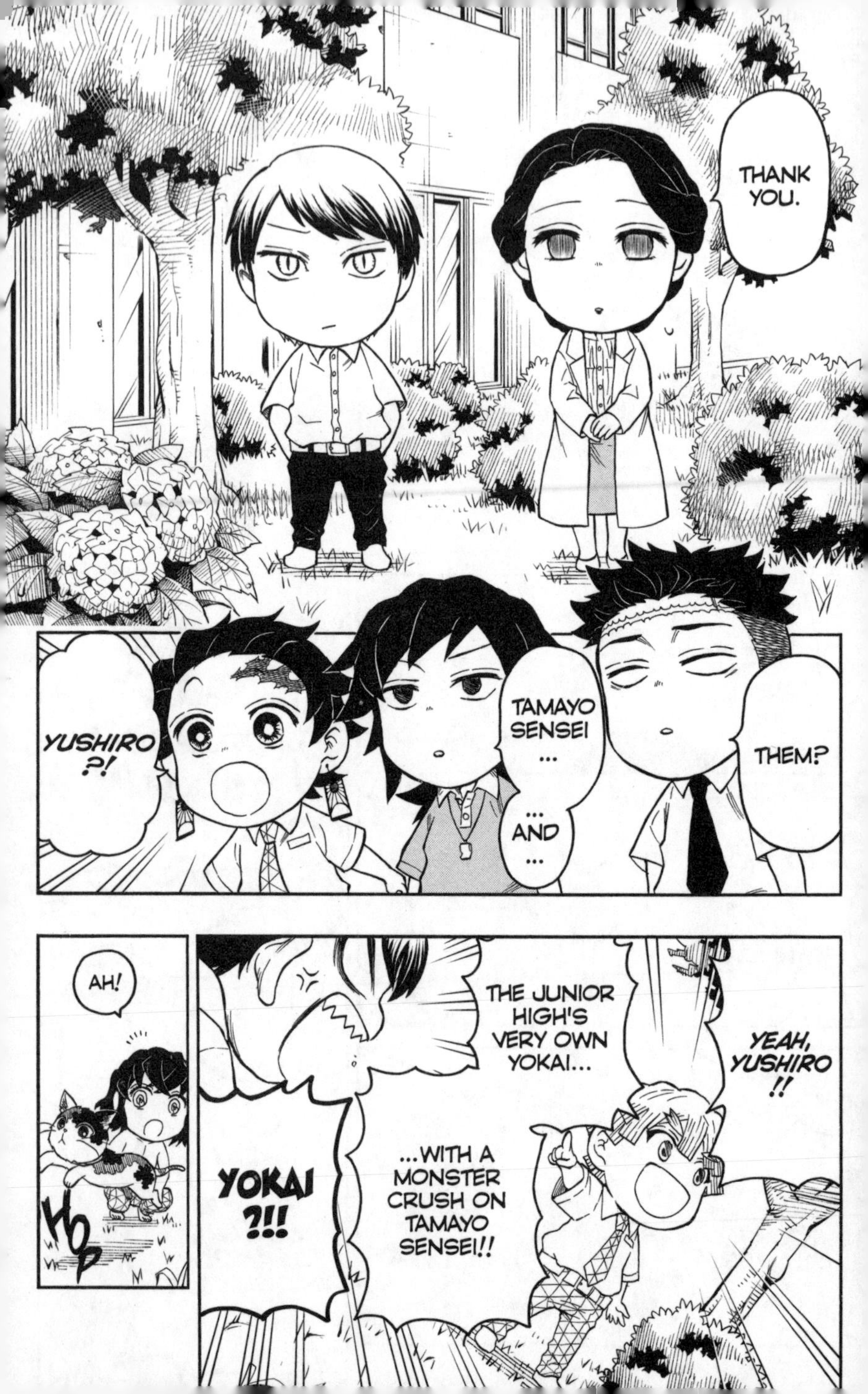
THANK YOU.
THEM?
TAMAYO SENSEI ...
... AND ...
YUSHIRO ?!
YEAH, YUSHIRO !!
THE JUNIOR HIGH'S VERY OWN YOKAI...
...WITH A MONSTER CRUSH ON TAMAYO SENSEI!!
YOKAI ?!!
AH!
HOP

WELL, UM...

IS THIS CAT YOURS?

CHACHA-MARU'S MY CAT.

I SAW YOUR POSTERS.

RUB RUB

...SO HE STARTED COMING EVERY DAY.

...AND HE TOOK A LIKING TO TAMAYO SENSEI...

I BROUGHT HIM TO SCHOOL ONE TIME...

YUSHIRO
GINKGO CLASS
JUNIOR HIGH, SECOND-YEAR

SO HIS NAME ISN'T ROCKY?

HMM...

OH, I SEE.

Sorry for all the trouble.

I CAN'T KEEP HIM IN THE NURSE'S OFFICE, SO I LET HIM OUTSIDE.

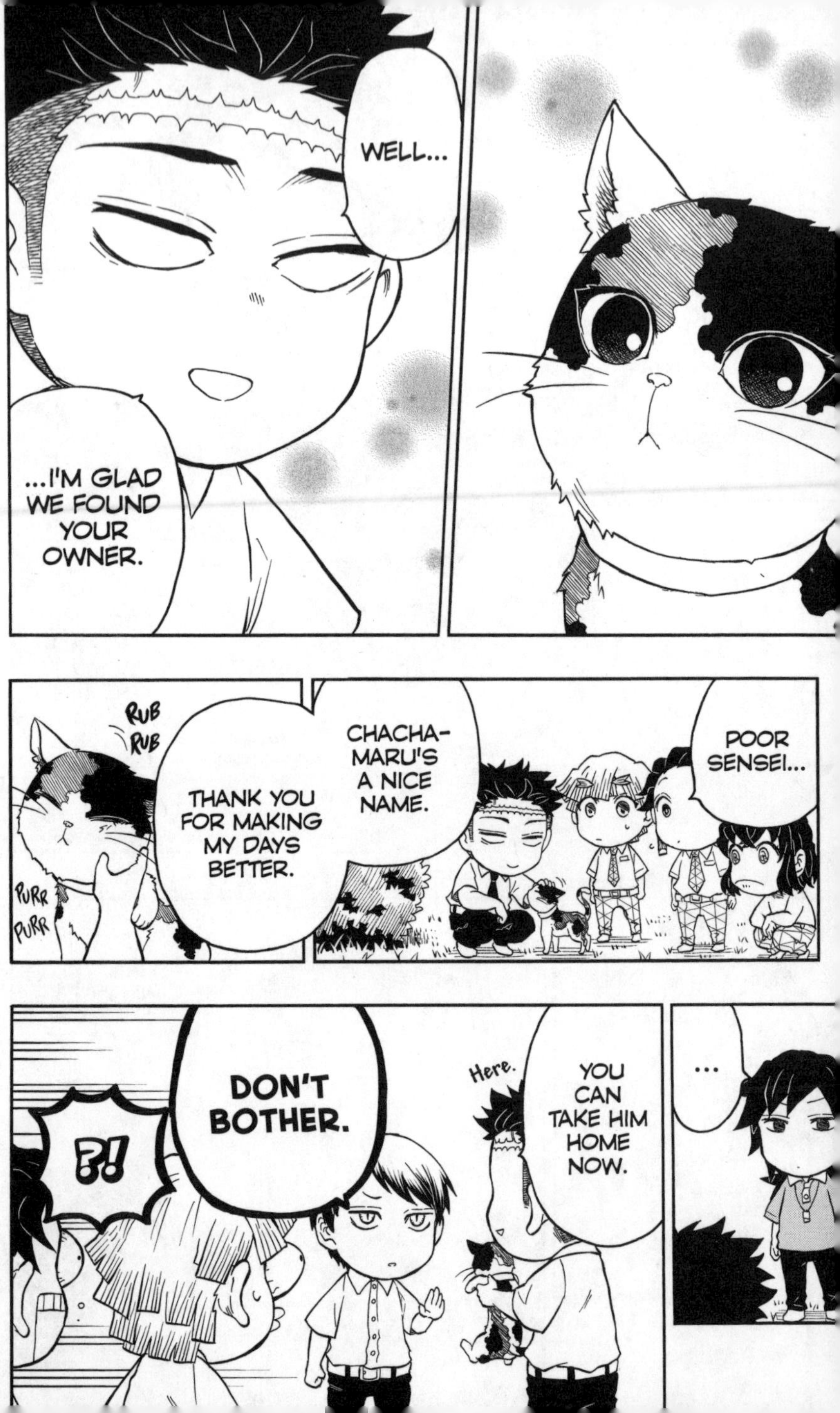
WELL...
...I'M GLAD WE FOUND YOUR OWNER.
POOR SENSEI...
CHACHA-MARU'S A NICE NAME.
THANK YOU FOR MAKING MY DAYS BETTER.
RUB RUB
PURR PURR
...
Here.
YOU CAN TAKE HIM HOME NOW.
DON'T BOTHER.
?!

SO WHY WERE YOU CHASING US AROUND?!

REALLY?!

TOMIOKA WAS LENIENT (FOR ONCE).

LOOK THIS WAY, SENSEI!

...HIMEJIMA PLAYING WITH CHACHAMARU AT SCHOOL.

...THE STUDENTS OFTEN SAW...

AFTER THAT...

No thanks.

Wanna pet him?

AND THAT'S WHY I KEEP TELLING YOU NOT TO RUN IN THE HALLS!

...COST QUITE A FEW BAGS OF DRIED SARDINES.

THAT SAID, REPLACING THE PHARMA-COLOGY CLUB'S SHELVES...

AWESOME ACADEMY

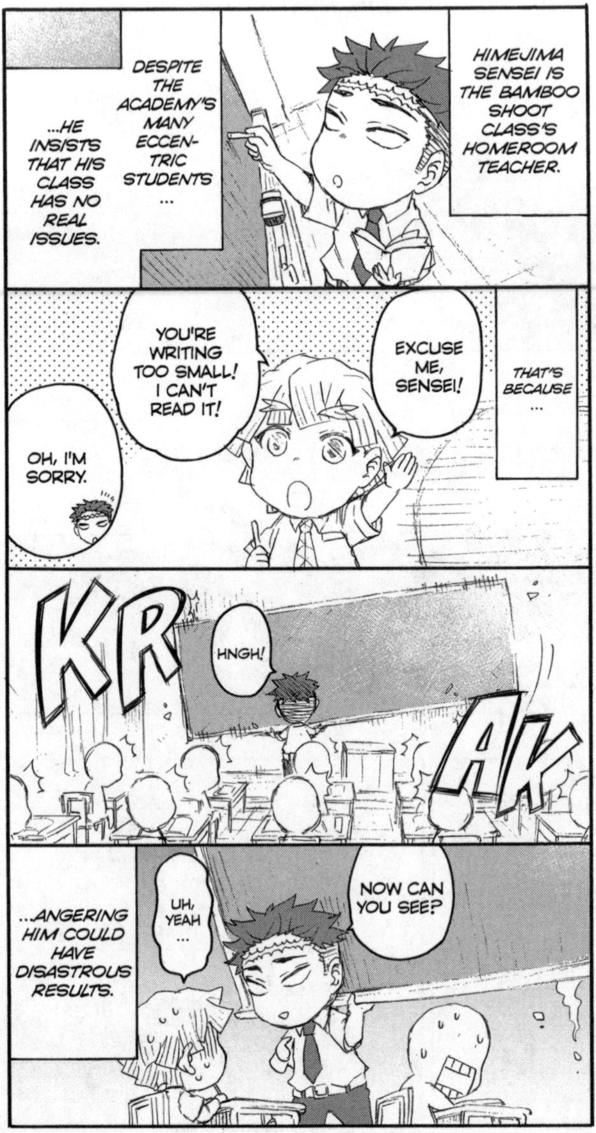
HIMEJIMA SENSEI IS THE BAMBOO SHOOT CLASS'S HOMEROOM TEACHER.
DESPITE THE ACADEMY'S MANY ECCENTRIC STUDENTS...
...HE INSISTS THAT HIS CLASS HAS NO REAL ISSUES.
THAT'S BECAUSE...
EXCUSE ME, SENSEI!
YOU'RE WRITING TOO SMALL! I CAN'T READ IT!
OH, I'M SORRY.
KR
HNGH!
AK
NOW CAN YOU SEE?
UH, YEAH...
...ANGERING HIM COULD HAVE DISASTROUS RESULTS.

But no one has ever seen him angry.

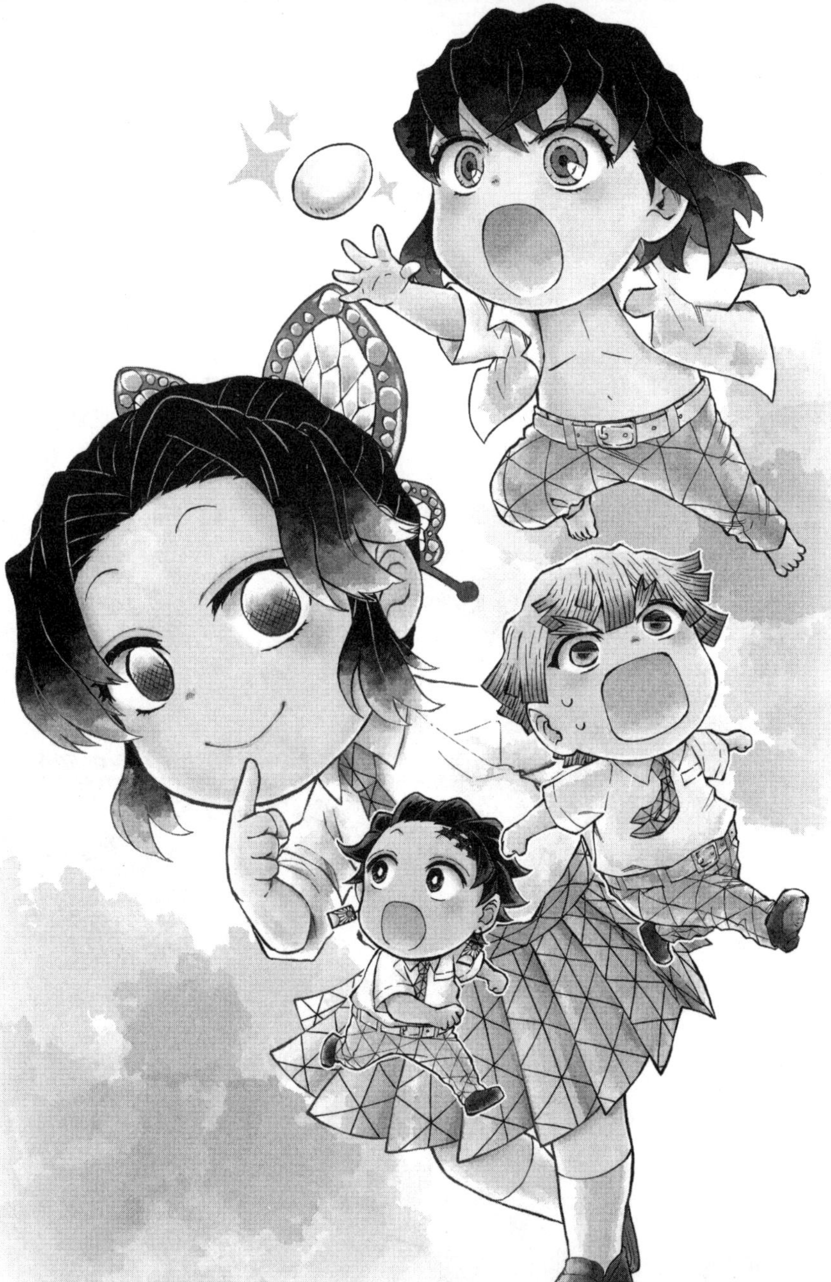

CHAPTER 7: THE SECRET OF HOT SPRING EGGS

OKAY, I'LL TAKE GOOD CARE OF MYSELF.

GOOD LUCK WITH YOUR SUMMER CLASSES.

OH, RIGHT!

DON'T PASS OUT FROM THE HEAT, HISA!

DRINK PLENTY OF WATER!!

I'LL BRING YOU BACK SOME HOT SPRING EGGS.

HOT SPRING EGGS?

YES, I'LL BRING A LOT.

SEE YOU SOON!

BETWEEN WORKING OUT AND SUMMER CLASSES...

...THIS ISN'T A BREAK AT ALL!

So hot!

UGH...

CH'IR CHIR CHIRR

ZENITSU AGATSUMA
BAMBOO SHOOT CLASS
FIRST-YEAR

WHAT ARE HOT SPRING EGGS?

HM?

AND ADDING HOMEWORK IN IS JUST CRUEL!

WHAT'S UP? WHY'RE YOU SO QUIET?

HEY, MONITSU?

SKREE SKREE

CHIR CHIR CHIRR CHIR CHIR

CH'IRR CHIR CHIR CHIRR

WHY?! CLASS IS ABOUT TO—

FORGET ABOUT CLASS!

NO QUESTIONS!! JUST COME OUT BACK WITH ME!!

WHAT WAS THAT FOR, ZENITSU?!

HE IS?!

INOSUKE'S IN DANGER!!

BUT INOSUKE DIDN'T KNOW WHAT THEY WERE...

...AND SAID SHE'D BRING BACK HOT SPRING EGGS!

TMP TMP TMP TMP TMP TMP TMP

W-WHAT HAP-PENED?!

HISA'S TAKING A TRIP TO A HOT SPRING...

...SO I TOLD HIM!!

"WHAT ARE HOT SPRING EGGS?"

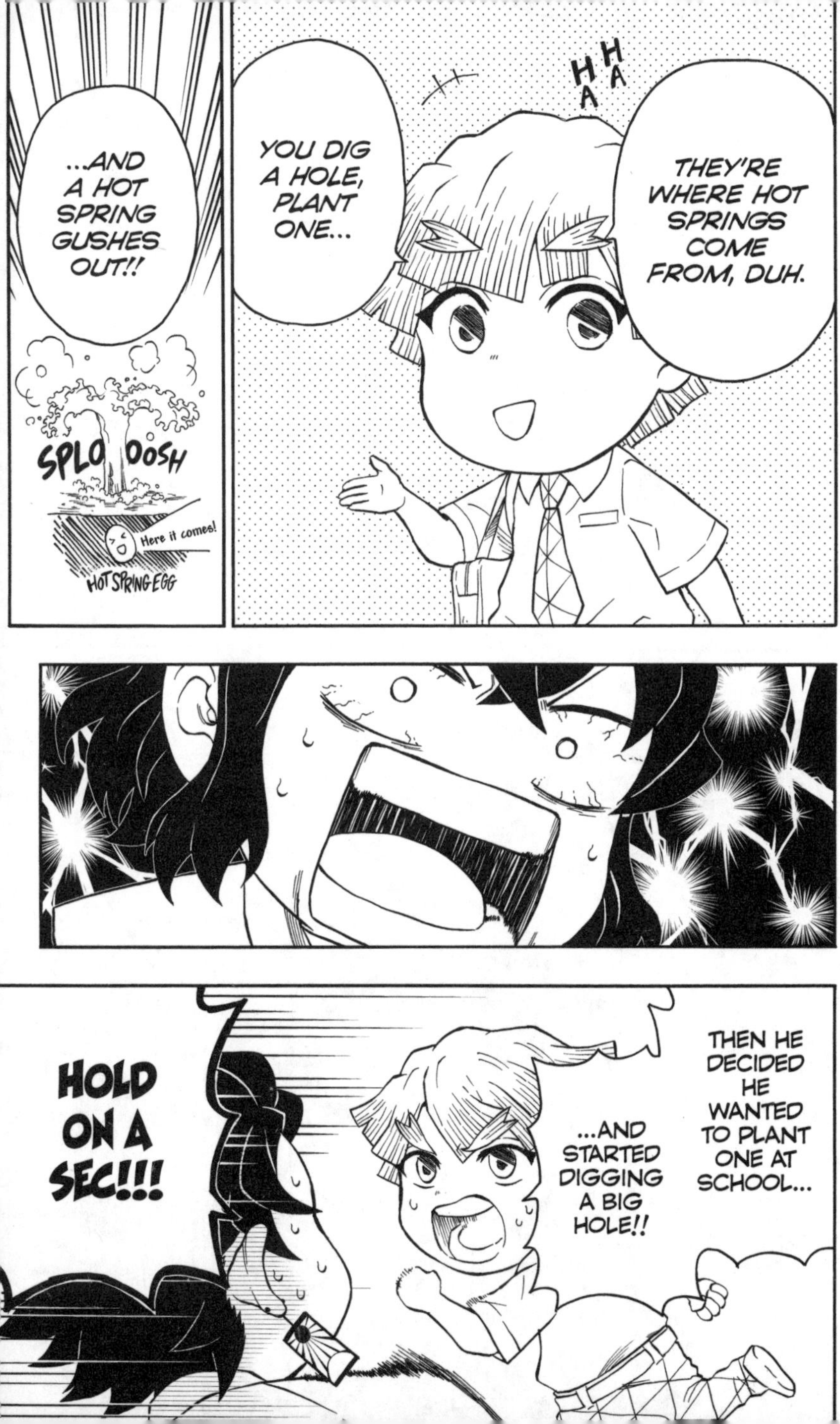
HA HA HA
THEY'RE WHERE HOT SPRINGS COME FROM, DUH.
YOU DIG A HOLE, PLANT ONE...
...AND A HOT SPRING GUSHES OUT!!
SPLOOOSH
Here it comes!
HOT SPRING EGG
THEN HE DECIDED HE WANTED TO PLANT ONE AT SCHOOL...
...AND STARTED DIGGING A BIG HOLE!!
HOLD ON A SEC!!!

AH HA HA! Oh you!!!!

CHAT CHAT

I DIDN'T THINK HE'D BELIEVE ME!

I THOUGHT IT'D BE MORE LIKE THIS!

—HOT SPRING EGGS (REAL)—
EGGS THAT HAVE BEEN BOILED SLOWLY AT LOW HEAT. YUM!

WHY'D YOU TELL HIM SUCH A STUPID LIE?!

?

GRAAH!

GRAAAAH!

WOOOSH

KIMETSU ACADEMY WESTERN GROUNDS

MOUNTAIN OUT BACK (FOOTHILLS)

CHIRR CHIRR CHIRR

WHEW!

THE BIGGER THE HOLE, THE BETTER, RIGHT?!

SHINK SHINK SHINK

...

HOT SPRING EGGS! HOT SPRING EGGS!

SHNK SHNK

...I'LL HAVE A GIANT HOT SPRING ALL READY FOR HER!

BY THE TIME HISA GETS BACK...

WHAT DO YOU MEAN?

NOW WHAT, TANJIRO?

DOES HE EVEN HAVE A BRAIN?

I THINK I'M GONNA CRY...

HE'S ACTUALLY DIGGING.

YOU WERE THE ONE WHO LIED TO HIM!!

...BUT I NEED YOU TO BE THE ONE TO TELL HIM THE TRUTH.

Listen... I'LL APOLO-GIZE LATER...

I'LL NEVER ASK ANOTHER FAVOR!

URGH...

NOW YOU GO APOLO-GIZE!

HOP TO IT!

WHAT?! HE'LL KILL ME!

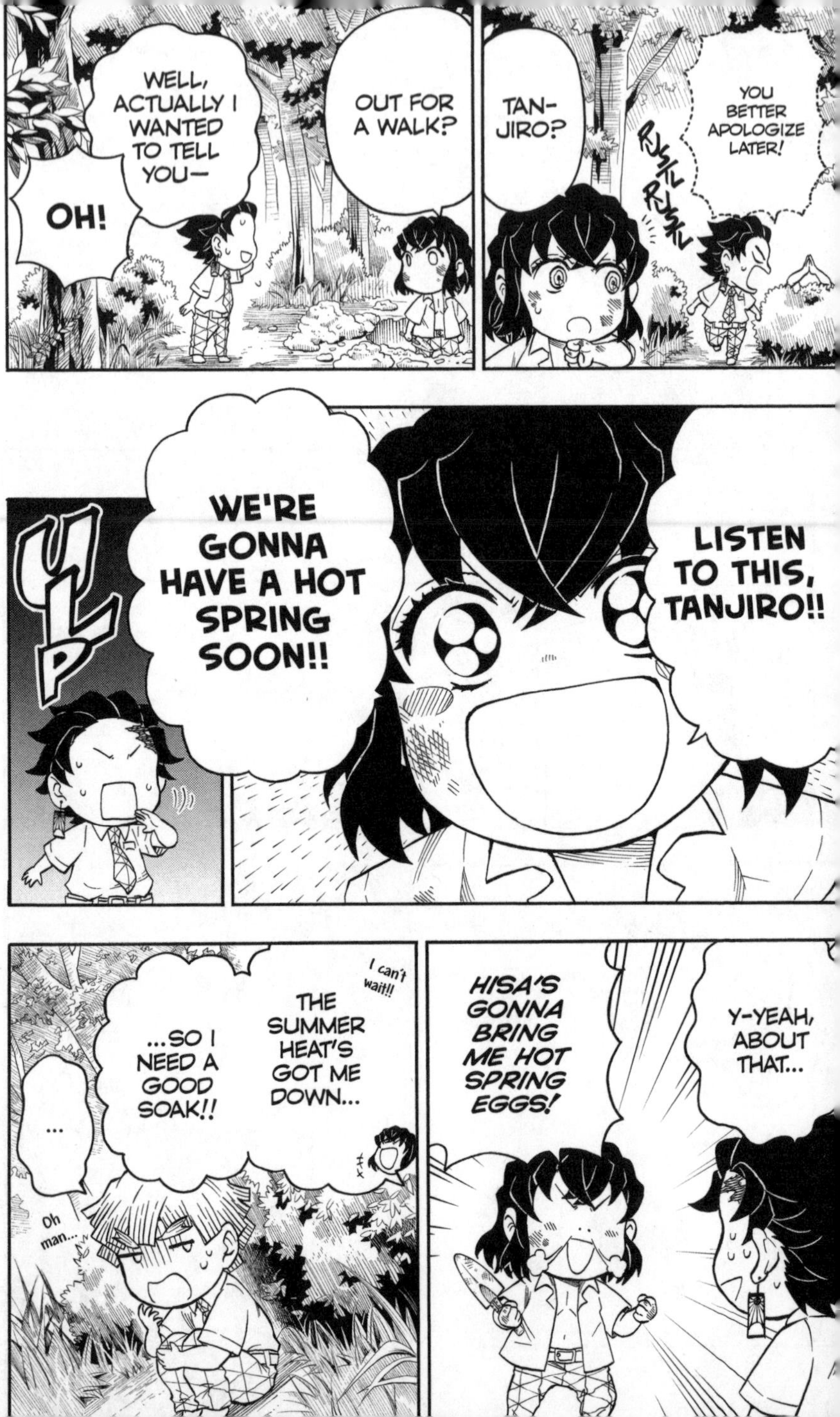
YOU BETTER APOLOGIZE LATER!
RUSTLE RUSTLE
TAN-JIRO?
OUT FOR A WALK?
WELL, ACTUALLY I WANTED TO TELL YOU—
OH!
LISTEN TO THIS, TANJIRO!!
WE'RE GONNA HAVE A HOT SPRING SOON!!
ULP
Y-YEAH, ABOUT THAT...
HISA'S GONNA BRING ME HOT SPRING EGGS!
I can't wait!!
THE SUMMER HEAT'S GOT ME DOWN...
...SO I NEED A GOOD SOAK!!
...
Oh man...

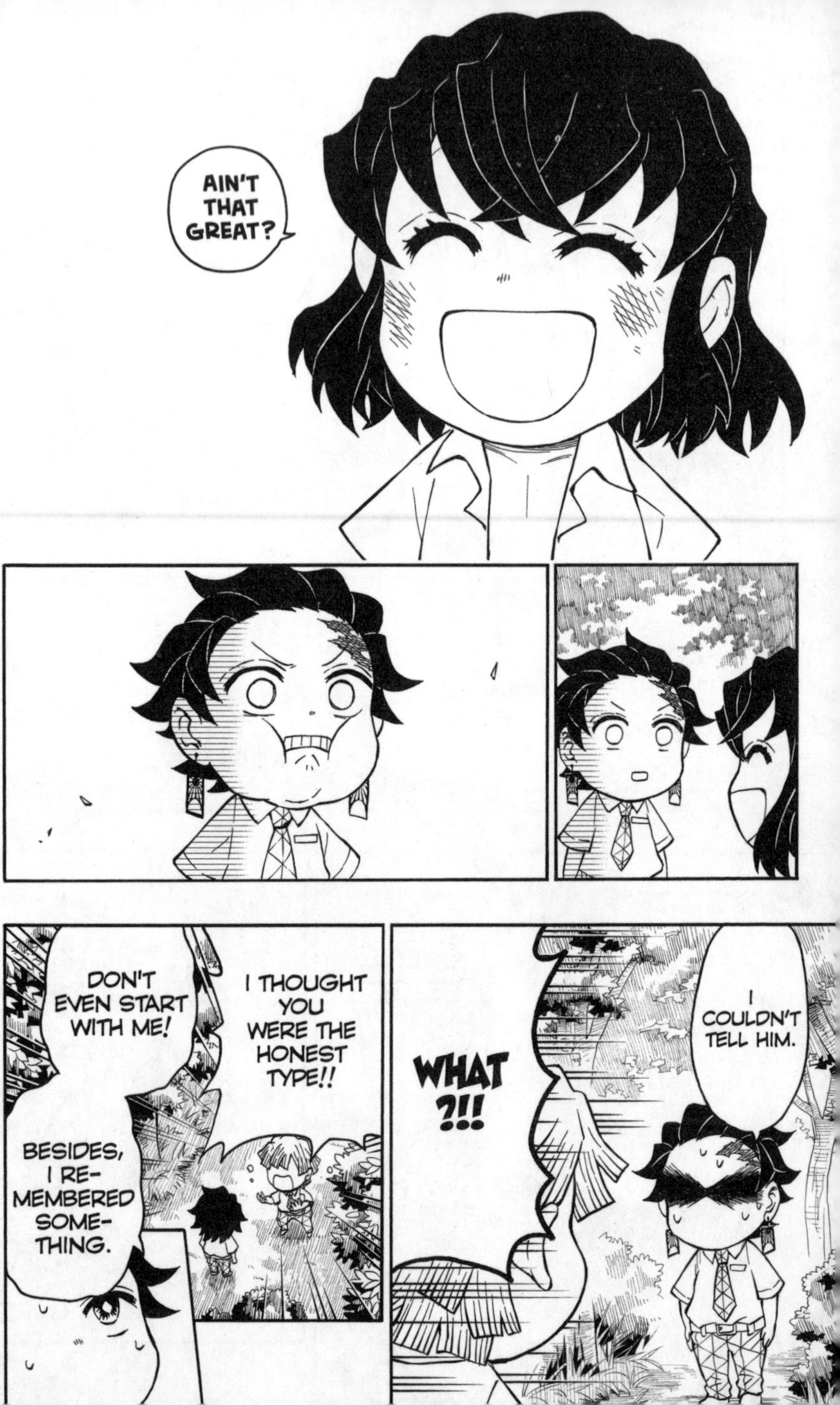
AIN'T THAT GREAT?
I COULDN'T TELL HIM.
WHAT ?!!
I THOUGHT YOU WERE THE HONEST TYPE!!
DON'T EVEN START WITH ME!
BESIDES, I RE-MEMBERED SOME-THING.

...TAKEO TOLD HER A BIG FIB.

TAKEO SAID A YOKAI INSIDE THE OVEN BAKES THE BREAD.

BACK WHEN HANAKO WAS LITTLE...

HANAKO
THE KAMADO FAMILY'S SECOND-OLDEST DAUGHTER

TAKEO
THE KAMADO FAMILY'S SECOND-OLDEST SON

BUT WHEN I TOLD HER THE TRUTH...

Yokai don't actually exist.

SHE WATCHED THE OVEN EVERY DAY, HOPING TO SEE THE YOKAI.

BA-BMP
BA-BMP

*TANJIRO'S FAMILY RUNS A BAKERY.

...SHE DIDN'T SPEAK TO ME FOR A WHOLE DAY!

PLIP
PLIP
PLIP

WANNA KNOW SOMETHING NEAT?

I DOUBT THAT!

HUH? NO, UM...

MAYBE WE'LL GET LUCKY AND ACTUALLY FIND ONE!

IT'S ENTIRELY POSSIBLE THERE COULD STILL BE SOME HIDING UNDER-GROUND.

...THIS AREA WAS KNOWN FOR ITS HOT SPRINGS.

BEFORE THEY BUILT THE SCHOOL ...

?!

AND VISIT A HOT SPRING AT SCHOOL?!

WE COULD ACTUALLY SUCCEED?!

KIMETSU HOT SPRING?!

THAT MEANS...

WAIT, REALLY ?!

YOU'VE NEVER HEARD OF...

...KIMETSU HOT SPRING?

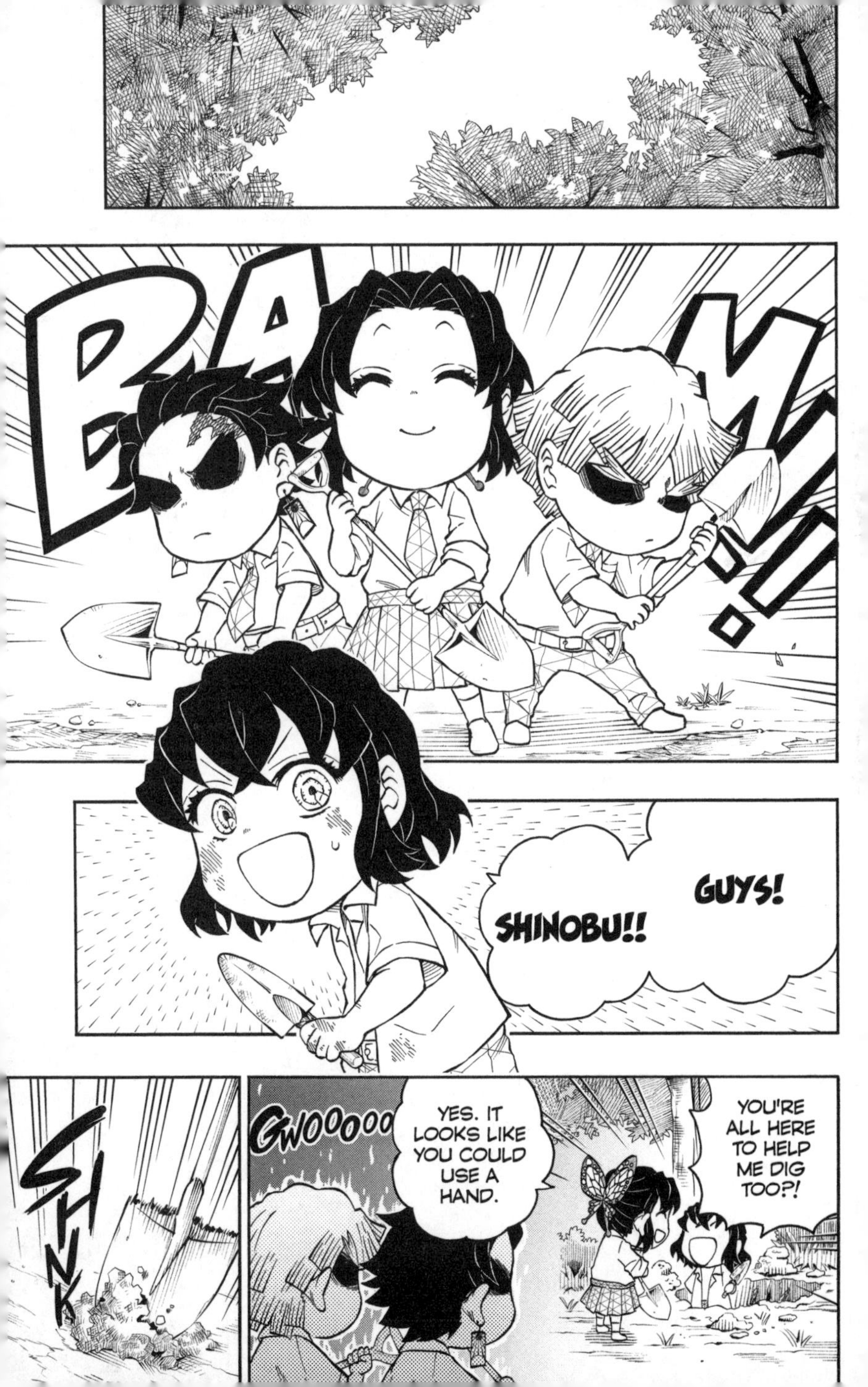
BAM!!
GUYS!
SHINOBU!!
YOU'RE ALL HERE TO HELP ME DIG TOO?!
YES. IT LOOKS LIKE YOU COULD USE A HAND.
GWOOOOO
SHUNK

URGH

THREE HOURS LATER...

GRRROWL

MAYBE WE NEED MINING GEAR?

NO! WE CAN'T GIVE UP!!

HUFF HUFF

STILL NO HOT SPRING...

NOT EVEN A DROP...

HUH? REALLY?!

HOW ABOUT LUNCH? MY TREAT!

IT'S ALMOST LUNCH TIME.

CLASSES SHOULD BE FINISHING SOON.

GROWWL

SO HUNGY...

WHEW! AT LEAST YOU FOUND US...

...AND NOT THEM.

THEM

WHAT'S THAT SUPPOSED TO MEAN?!

GAH! THERE YOU ARE!!

YOU'VE BEEN DITCHING CLASS!!

FORGOT ABOUT THAT. Oops.

I'LL GO GET US SOME DRINKS!

CHIRR CHIRR CHIRR CHIRR

WELL, IF YOU SAY SO.

Really?

SORRY. I NEEDED THEIR HELP WITH SOMETHING.

I'LL CLEAR IT LATER.

NOW LET'S EAT!!

A HOT SPRING WILL MAKE HER HAPPY TOO!

PSST PSST PSST

I FEEL BAD ABOUT THIS, BUT...

FEEL FREE TO EAT!

OKAY!

PIWOK

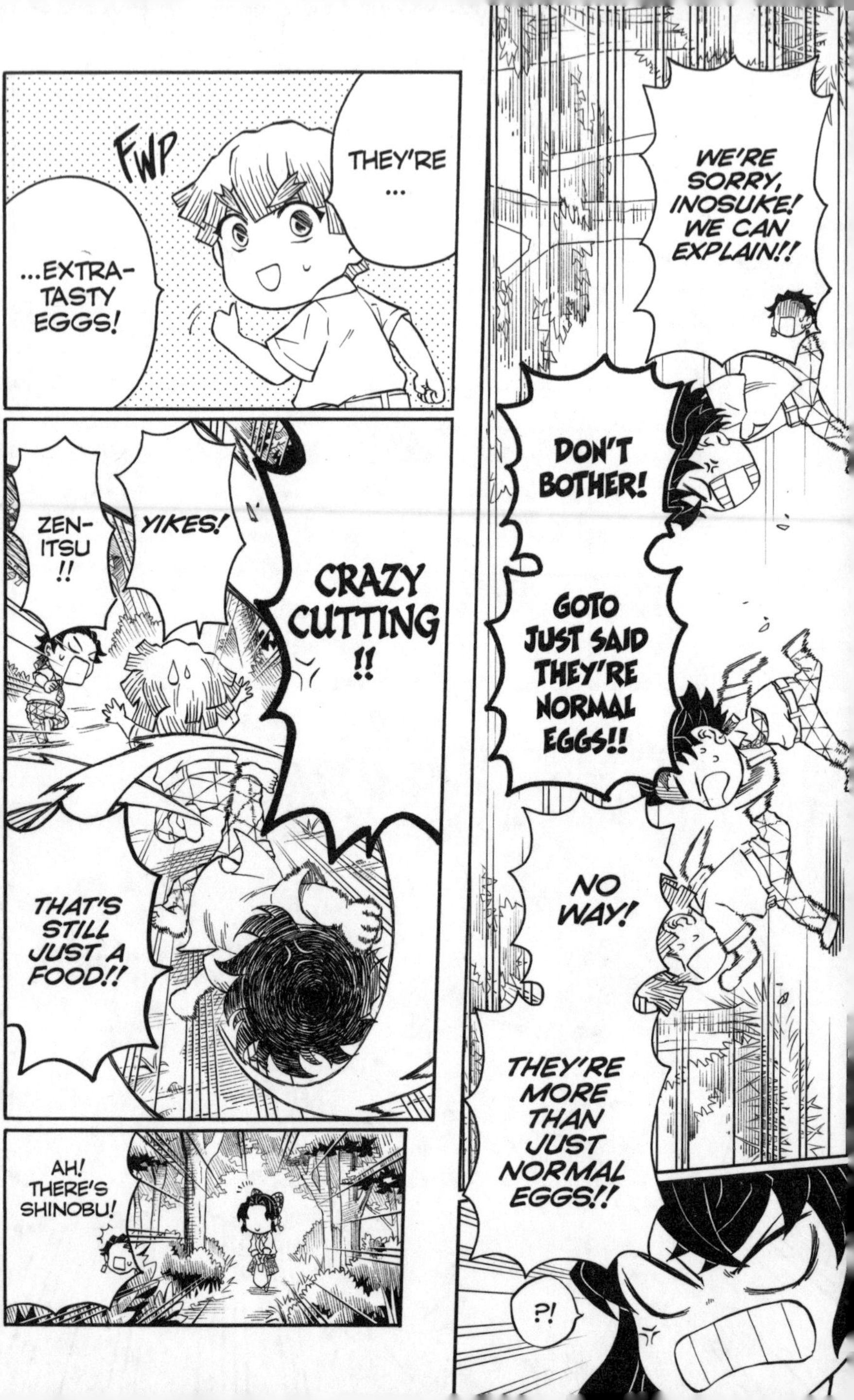
WE'RE SORRY, INOSUKE! WE CAN EXPLAIN!!
DON'T BOTHER!
GOTO JUST SAID THEY'RE NORMAL EGGS!!
NO WAY!
THEY'RE MORE THAN JUST NORMAL EGGS!!
?!
THEY'RE ...
FWP
...EXTRA-TASTY EGGS!
YIKES!
ZEN-ITSU!!
CRAZY CUTTING!!
THAT'S STILL JUST A FOOD!!
AH! THERE'S SHINOBU!

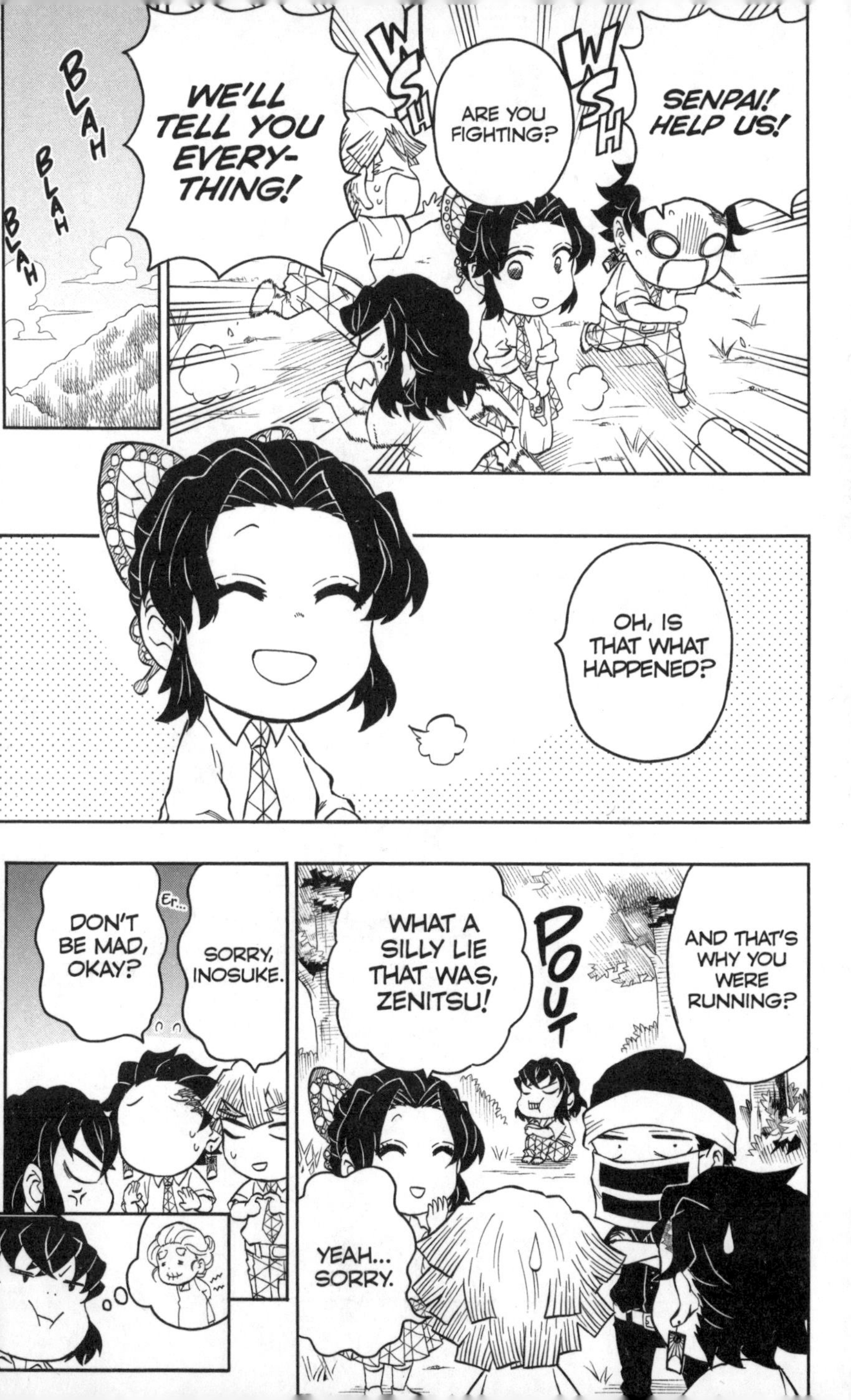
SENPAI! HELP US!
WSH
ARE YOU FIGHTING?
WSH
WE'LL TELL YOU EVERY-THING!
BLAH
BLAH
BLAH
OH, IS THAT WHAT HAPPENED?
AND THAT'S WHY YOU WERE RUNNING?
POUT
WHAT A SILLY LIE THAT WAS, ZENITSU!
YEAH... SORRY.
SORRY, INOSUKE.
Er...
DON'T BE MAD, OKAY?

WE'RE REALLY, REALLY ... SORRY !!

FWAAAA

INOSUKE ...

COLD

TCH

NO TEA

THEY'RE A NATURAL OCCUR- ANCE...

...THAT ONLY APPEAR IN CERTAIN PLACES.

THAT'S WHY THEY'RE SO VALUABLE.

...HOT SPRINGS OCCUR...

...WHEN GEOTHERMAL ACTIVITY HEATS GROUNDWATER.

HOT SPRING

GROUNDWATER

HERE YOU GO!!

MAGMA

THEY'RE GOOD FOR BACK PAIN!

Club prez ↓

BATH SALTS THE PHARMACOLOGY CLUB MADE!

WHAT'S INSIDE?

REALLY?!

TAKE THIS AS THANKS!

BUTTERFLY BRAND

SWUP

I'LL BE GOING NOW.

SHE KNEW WE WERE LYING?!

No way!

HUH?

SHE HAD THAT PREPARED.

...

WHAT ABOUT KIMETSU HOT SPRING?

We'll help!

DON'T YOU WANT TO FIND A HOT SPRING?

ARE YOU GOING TO KEEP DIGGING?

NO. I'M LEAVING AFTER I EAT.

WHAT?!

WHAT'RE YOU TALKING ABOUT?

DON'T LEAVE IT TO HER

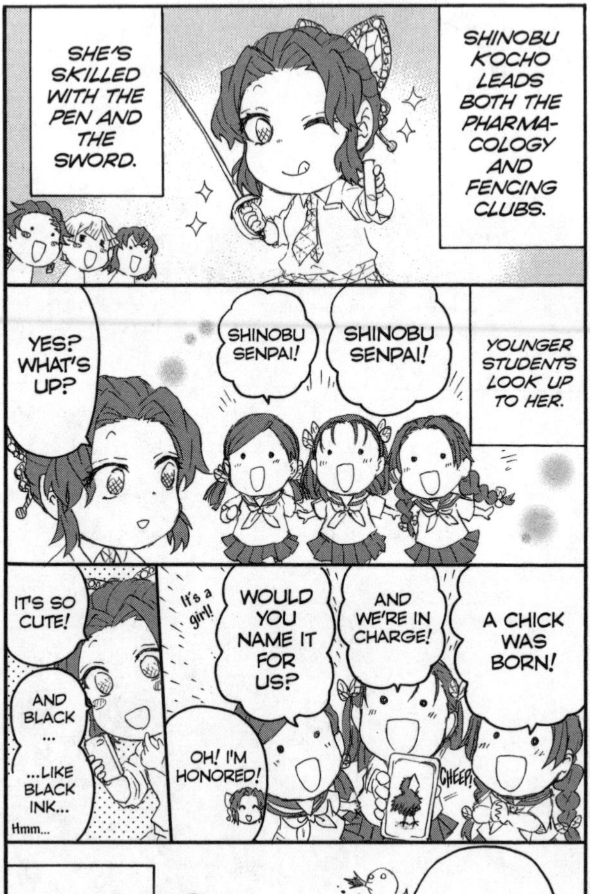
SHINOBU KOCHO LEADS BOTH THE PHARMA-COLOGY AND FENCING CLUBS.
SHE'S SKILLED WITH THE PEN AND THE SWORD.
YOUNGER STUDENTS LOOK UP TO HER.
SHINOBU SENPAI!
SHINOBU SENPAI!
YES? WHAT'S UP?
A CHICK WAS BORN!
CHEEP!
AND WE'RE IN CHARGE!
WOULD YOU NAME IT FOR US?
It's a girl!
OH! I'M HONORED!
IT'S SO CUTE!
AND BLACK ...
...LIKE BLACK INK...
Hmm...
CHIC-TOPUS!
BUT SHE SUCKS AT NAMING THINGS.

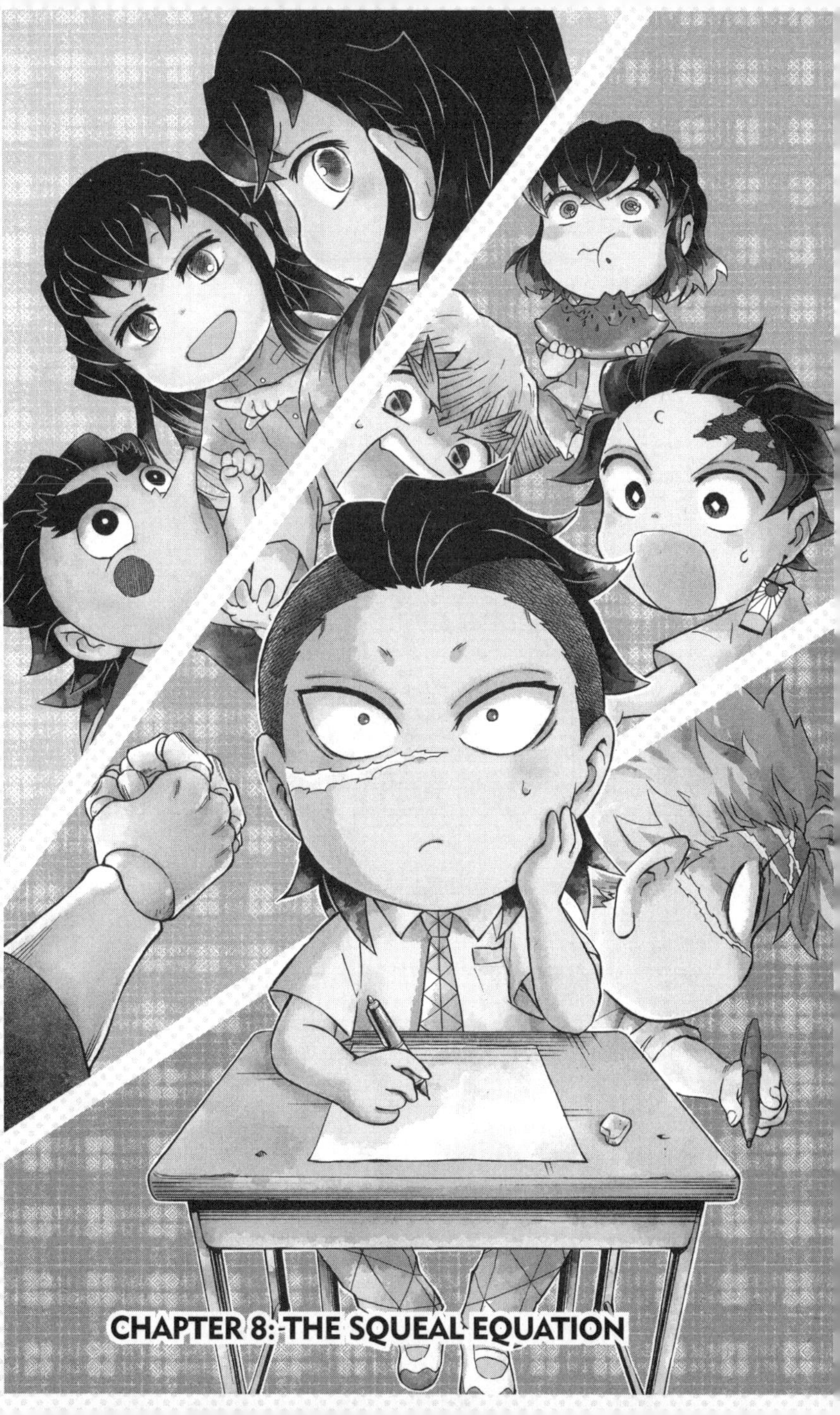
CHAPTER 8: THE SQUEAL EQUATION

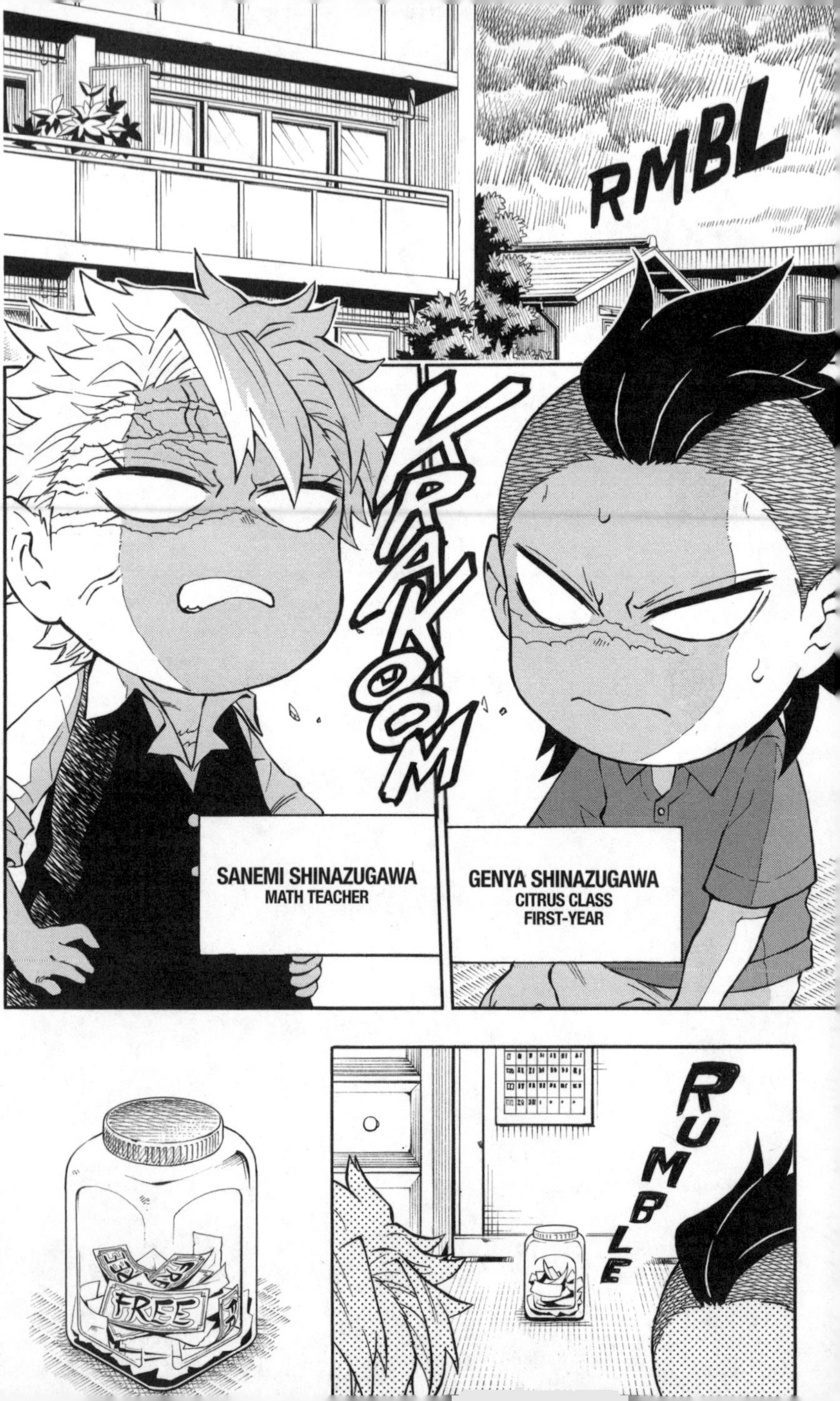
RMBL
VRAKOOM
GENYA SHINAZUGAWA
CITRUS CLASS
FIRST-YEAR
SANEMI SHINAZUGAWA
MATH TEACHER
RUMBLE
FREE

WE HAD A FIGHT ABOUT MY GRADES!!

I CAN'T ASK HIM!

MY FINAL EXAM SCORES SUCKED!

WHAT HAPPENED?

YOU CAN FIGHT HIM? RESPECT!

GOT THAT, GENYA?

IF YOU SCORE THIS BADLY AGAIN...

NEVER SCORE THIS LOW AGAIN!

FLASH-BACK

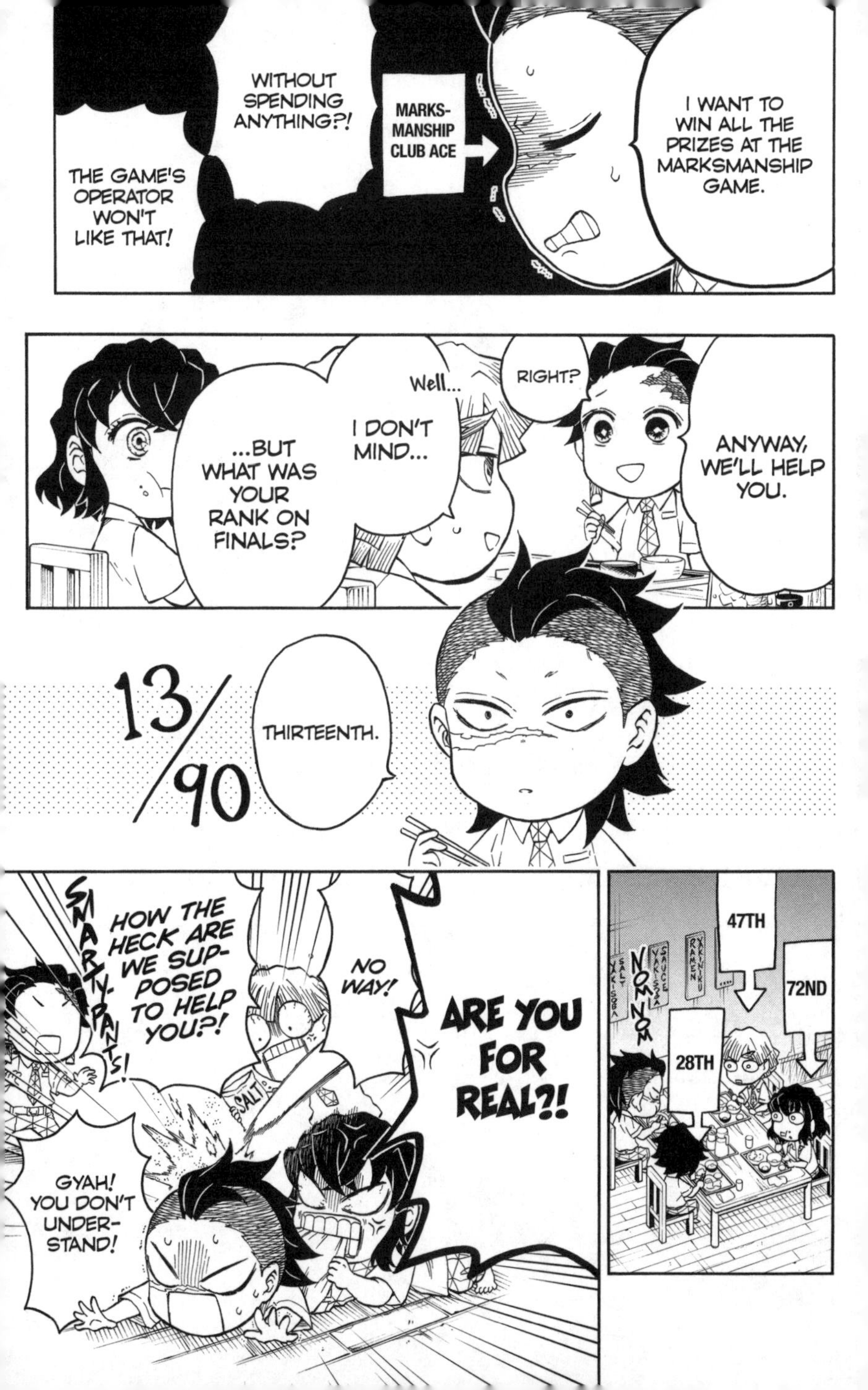
I WANT TO WIN ALL THE PRIZES AT THE MARKSMANSHIP GAME.
MARKS-MANSHIP CLUB ACE
WITHOUT SPENDING ANYTHING?!
THE GAME'S OPERATOR WON'T LIKE THAT!
ANYWAY, WE'LL HELP YOU.
RIGHT?
Well...
I DON'T MIND...
...BUT WHAT WAS YOUR RANK ON FINALS?
THIRTEENTH.
13/90
47TH
72ND
YAKINIKU
RAMEN
SAUCE YAKISOBA
SALT YAKISOBA
NOM NOM
28TH
ARE YOU FOR REAL?!
NO WAY!
HOW THE HECK ARE WE SUP-POSED TO HELP YOU?!
SMARTYPANTS!
SALT
GYAH! YOU DON'T UNDER-STAND!

SORRY, AOI!

ACK!

JOLT

PIPE DOWN OVER THERE!!

AOI KANZAKI
PERSIMMON CLASS
SECOND-YEAR
(AOZORA DINER
EMPLOYEE)

WELL NOW I'M JUST OFFENDED.

JUST POINT ME AT SOMEONE WHO CAN!

...SO I KNOW YOU CAN'T HELP ME!

IT WAS MY MATH SCORES THAT WERE THE PROBLEM...

PSST

NOT HER, IDIOT!!

HEY, AOI!!

LET'S ASK AOI!!

HOW ABOUT AN OLDER STUDENT?

REFILL PLEASE.

YES, INOSUKE?

SO...NOT KANAO OR SHINOBU?

KANAO

SHINOBU

PICK A GUY!

NO GIRLS!

NERVOUS AROUND GIRLS

HMM

HE'S AWAY AT SOCCER CAMP.

SPARKL

HOW ABOUT MURATA?

6

TOKITO

DING DONG

I KNOW!

IT DOESN'T HAVE TO BE AN *OLDER* STUDENT!

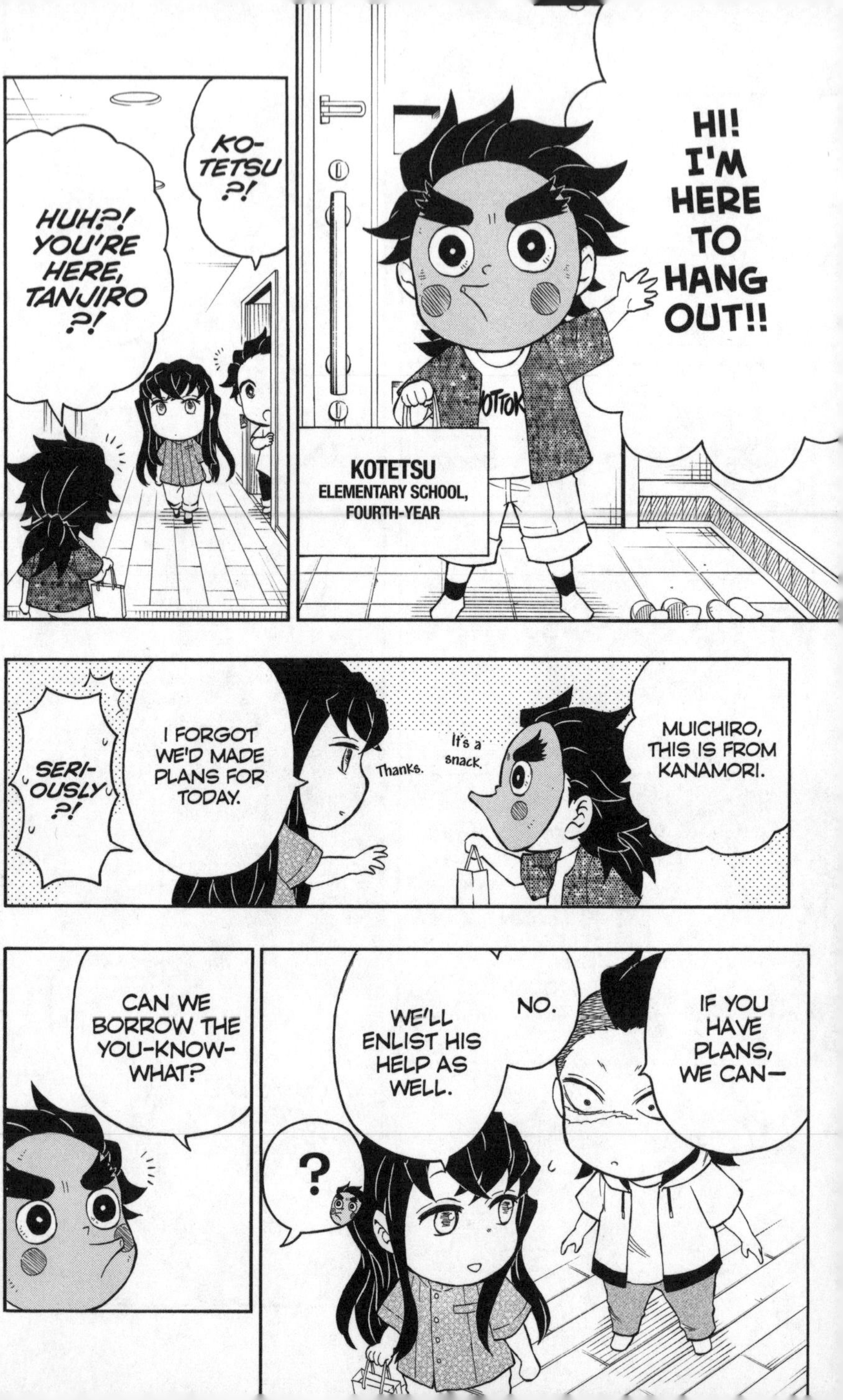
HI! I'M HERE TO HANG OUT!!
KOTETSU
ELEMENTARY SCHOOL,
FOURTH-YEAR
KO-TETSU?!
HUH?! YOU'RE HERE, TANJIRO?!
MUICHIRO, THIS IS FROM KANAMORI.
It's a snack.
Thanks.
I FORGOT WE'D MADE PLANS FOR TODAY.
SERI-OUSLY?!
IF YOU HAVE PLANS, WE CAN—
NO.
WE'LL ENLIST HIS HELP AS WELL.
?
CAN WE BORROW THE YOU-KNOW-WHAT?

I'D BE DEAD!!!

IT'S GOOD FOR MOTIVATION.

* WATERMELON

...THAT'LL BE YOUR HEAD.

THAT WOULD KILL ME!!

AND WHAT'D YOU DO TO ITS HANDS?!

THAT'S NOT JUST A DOLL, THEN!

YOU PROGRAM IT?!

TAK TAK TAK TAK

I'LL PROGRAM IT TO STOP FOR CORRECT ANSWERS.

HOW IS THAT GONNA MOTIVATE ME?!

I have plenty.

WE'LL JUST HAVE IT SPLIT ANOTHER WATERMELON INSTEAD.

FROM TETSUIDO

TOKITO, I THINK THIS IS A LITTLE TOO DANGEROUS.

OH, OKAY.

...AFTER THE DOLL SPLITS THE WATERMELON...

...I'LL HAVE NO CHOICE BUT TO THROW AWAY THE LEFTOVERS.

OKAY, IN THAT CASE...

CHOMP MUNCH CHOMP

AT THAT POINT YOU'RE JUST WASTING WATERMELON!!

LOVES WATERMELON

IF THAT'S ALL IT TAKES, WHY'RE WE EVEN USING THAT THING?!

GRAAAAAH

I CAN'T LET THAT HAPPEN!!

THAT'D BE TERRIBLE!!

UM...

...BE STUDYING TOO?

SHOULDN'T YOU THREE...

HUH?

DOESN'T THAT WORRY YOU?

YOUR GRADES ARE WORSE THAN HIS, RIGHT?

YOU GET BAD GRADES WHEN YOU'RE LAZY.

HARSH

TICK TICK TICK

YOU HAVE 20 SECONDS!!

$$y = -3(x-1)^2 + 5$$
$$-3 \leqq x \leqq -1$$

FIND THE MAXIMUM AND MINIMUM VALUES FOR THIS EQUATION!!

FIRST QUESTION!!

W-WELL, UM...

UM...X=-3 FOR A MINIMUM OF -43 AND X=-1 FOR A MAX OF -7!!!

...

COR-RECT!

BESIDES, YORIICHI IS BUSY WITH GENYA.

CHOP

GAH!

DURING SUMMER BREAK IT IS WISE TO STUDY HARD BUT WHO WOULD BOTHER?

—A SUMMER HAIKU BY THREE NINCOMPOOPS

TING TING

GENYA'S DEDI-CATED!

I'M NOT GETTING PUNCHED BY THAT THING!

NO WAY!

GAH!

I DIALED IT DOWN TO GOOSE-EGG MODE.

NO WORRIES! I'VE GOT ANOTHER ONE!!

UH-OH!!

OH, BIG BRO'S HOME!

C'MON, GUYS! STUDY!

QUIET DOWN OVER THERE!

I'M HOME!

WHAT'S ALL THE EXCITE-MENT?

WELCOME HOME, YUICHIRO!!

CAN YOU HELP US STUDY?!

YUICHIRO TOKITO
GINKGO CLASS
JUNIOR HIGH, SECOND-YEAR

?!

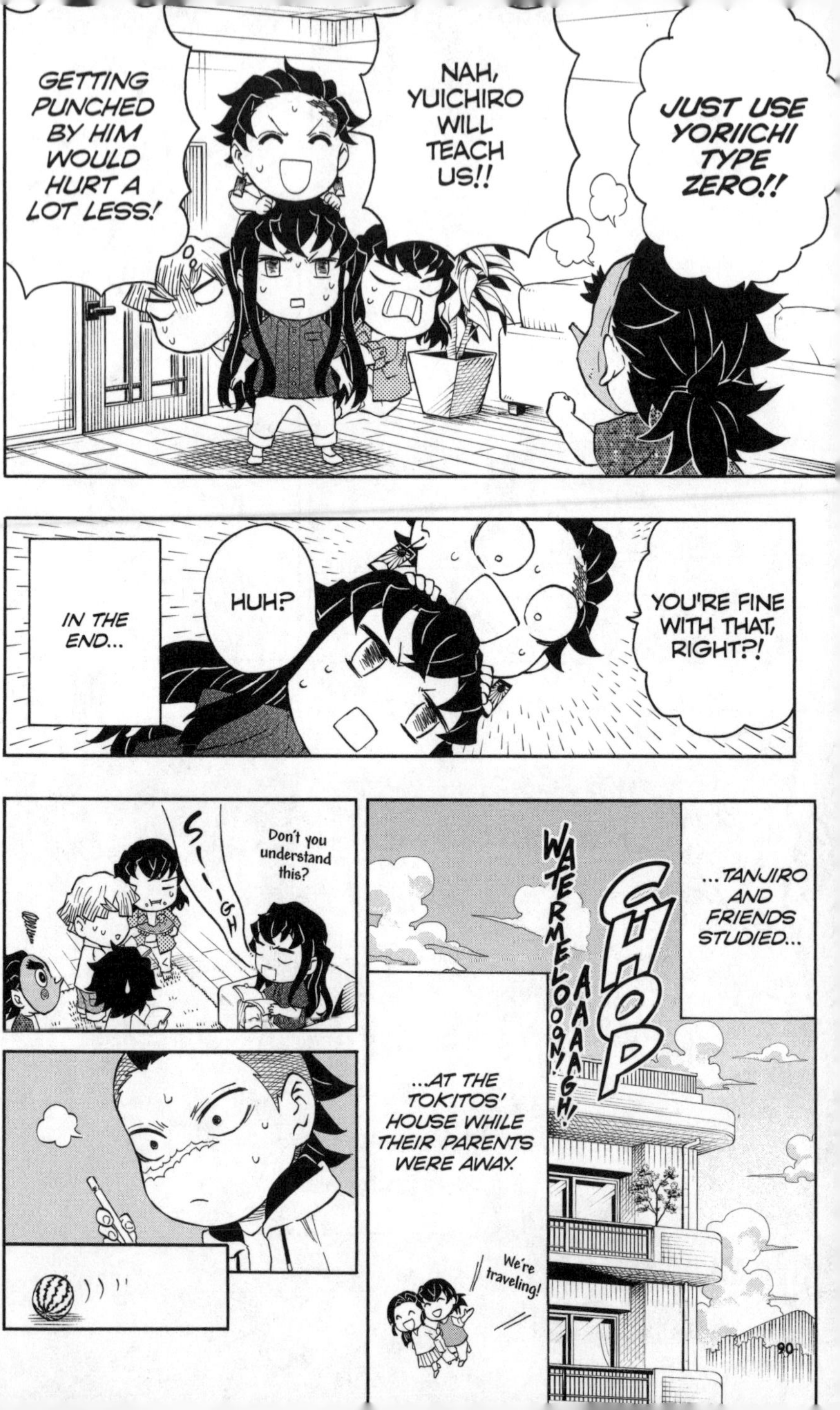
JUST USE YORIICHI TYPE ZERO!!
NAH, YUICHIRO WILL TEACH US!!
GETTING PUNCHED BY HIM WOULD HURT A LOT LESS!
YOU'RE FINE WITH THAT, RIGHT?!
HUH?
IN THE END...
...TANJIRO AND FRIENDS STUDIED...
CHOP
WATERMELOOON! AAAAGH!
...AT THE TOKITOS' HOUSE WHILE THEIR PARENTS WERE AWAY.
We're traveling!
Don't you understand this?
SIIIGH

RATL

PIP

TAKING A BREAK, GENYA?

YEAH.

WE'RE GONNA ORDER PIZZA.

KOTETSU'S RELATIVES RUN A PIZZA JOINT.

Part-time delivery girl Mitsuru

SOUNDS GREAT!!

BLEH...

I WAS HOPING I COULD SPEND THE NIGHT TONIGHT...

...SO ABOUT TOMORROW'S BREAD...

REALLY? THANKS, MOM!

I KNOW THAT'S THE RIGHT ATTITUDE, BUT...

Y-YEAH...

LET'S ALL DO OUR BEST!!

DON'T WORRY! YOU'LL GET YOUR VOUCHERS BACK!!

?

HE'S LIKE AN INFORMATION SPONGE.

YOU THINK SO?

...I CAN'T BELIEVE THAT TOKITO...

...ALREADY KNOWS ALL THIS.

IF I WAS GIFTED LIKE TOKITO...

GRRR

You try it!

Come on already!

STAY BACK! YIIIKES!

CHATTER

Goose-egg mode

C'mon! Just try it!

CHATTER

...THEN MY BROTHER WOULDN'T GET MAD AT ME...

...FOR BEING A LOSER.

HE MUST BE ASHAMED OF ME.

CONTEMPLATIVE

GENYA...

...YOU'RE NOT A LOSER.

HIS FAVO-RITE?!

YOU'RE HIS FAVORITE!

HE GETS ANGRY BECAUSE HE CARES ABOUT YOU.

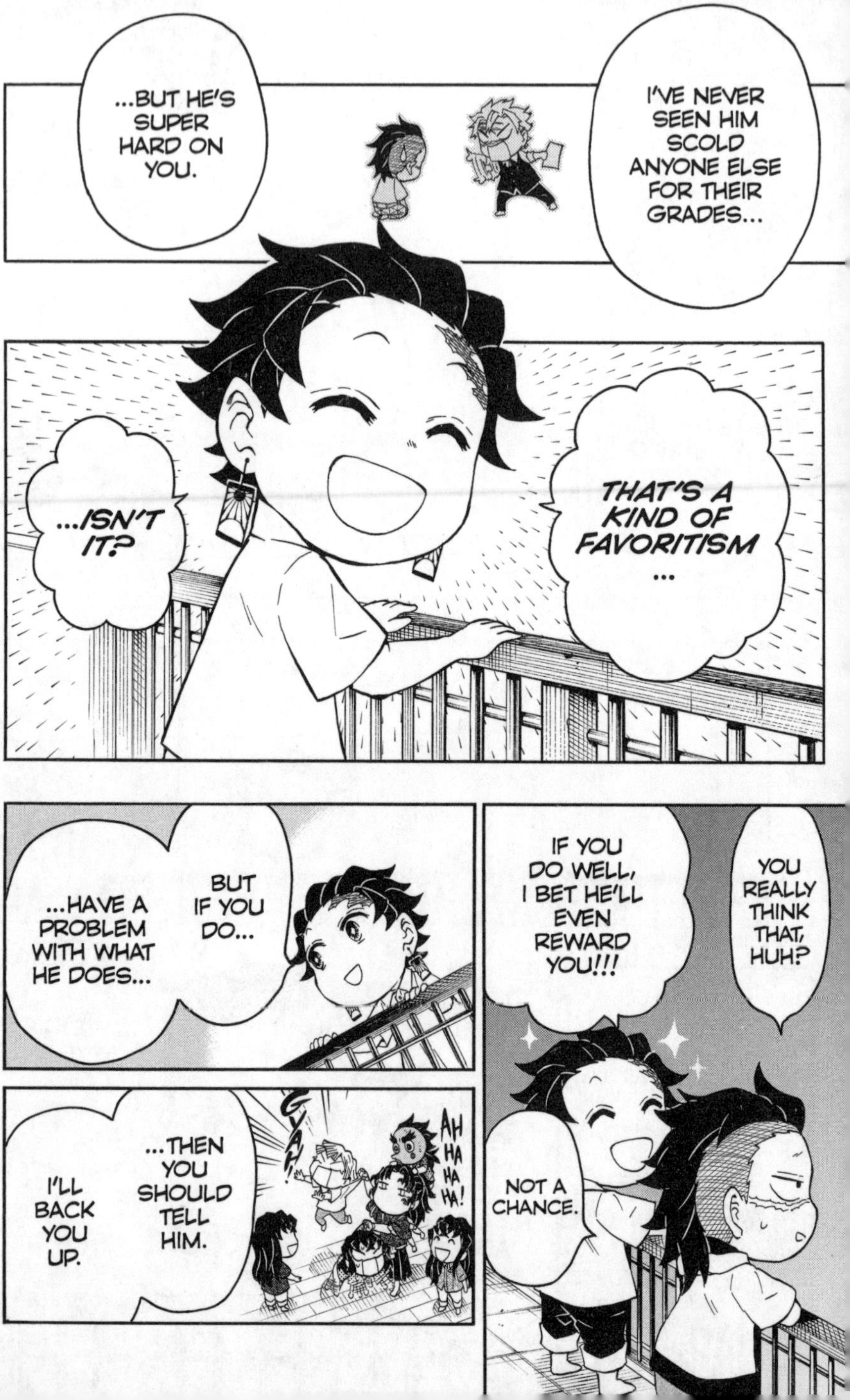
I'VE NEVER SEEN HIM SCOLD ANYONE ELSE FOR THEIR GRADES...
...BUT HE'S SUPER HARD ON YOU.
THAT'S A KIND OF FAVORITISM ...
...ISN'T IT?
YOU REALLY THINK THAT, HUH?
IF YOU DO WELL, I BET HE'LL EVEN REWARD YOU!!!
NOT A CHANCE.
BUT IF YOU DO...
...HAVE A PROBLEM WITH WHAT HE DOES...
AH HA HA HA HA!
GYAH!
...THEN YOU SHOULD TELL HIM.
I'LL BACK YOU UP.

QUIT CHATTING AND HELLLLLP !!!

...I'M GOING TO DO MY BEST.

Great!

OKAY.

BUT FIRST...

CHATTER

CHATTER

CHATTER

TEST DAY...

BA-BMP

BA-BMP

"THAT'S A KIND OF FAVORIT-ISM!"

EVERY-ONE GOT A TEST?

WE'RE STARTING IN 30 SECONDS!

FWP FWP FWP

CHATTER

CHATTER

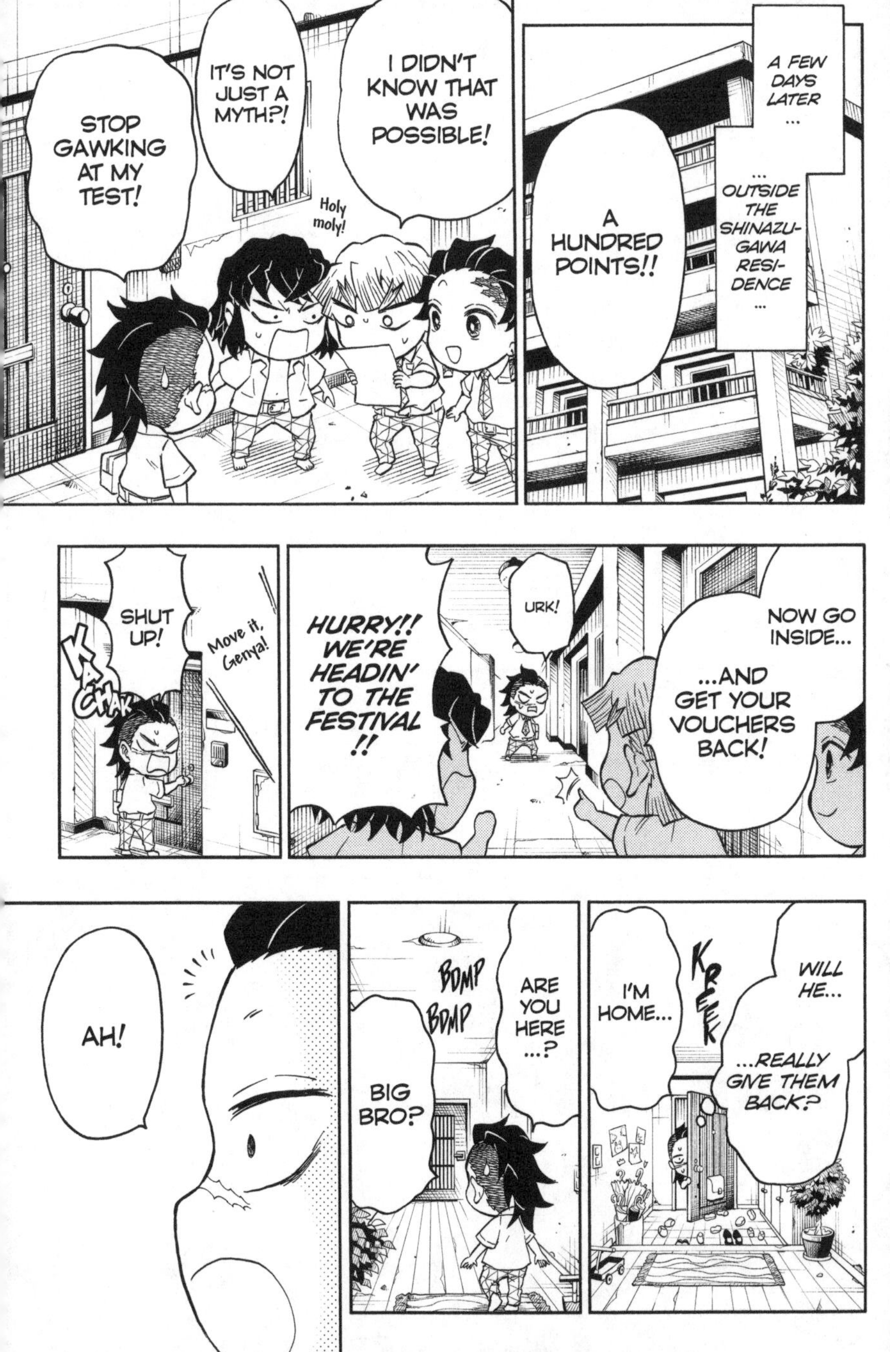
A FEW DAYS LATER ...
... OUTSIDE THE SHINAZUGAWA RESIDENCE ...
A HUNDRED POINTS!!
I DIDN'T KNOW THAT WAS POSSIBLE!
IT'S NOT JUST A MYTH?!
Holy moly!
STOP GAWKING AT MY TEST!
NOW GO INSIDE...
...AND GET YOUR VOUCHERS BACK!
URK!
HURRY!! WE'RE HEADIN' TO THE FESTIVAL!!
Move it, Genya!
SHUT UP!
KACHAK
WILL HE...
...REALLY GIVE THEM BACK?
KREEK
I'M HOME...
ARE YOU HERE ...?
BDMP BDMP
BIG BRO?
AH!

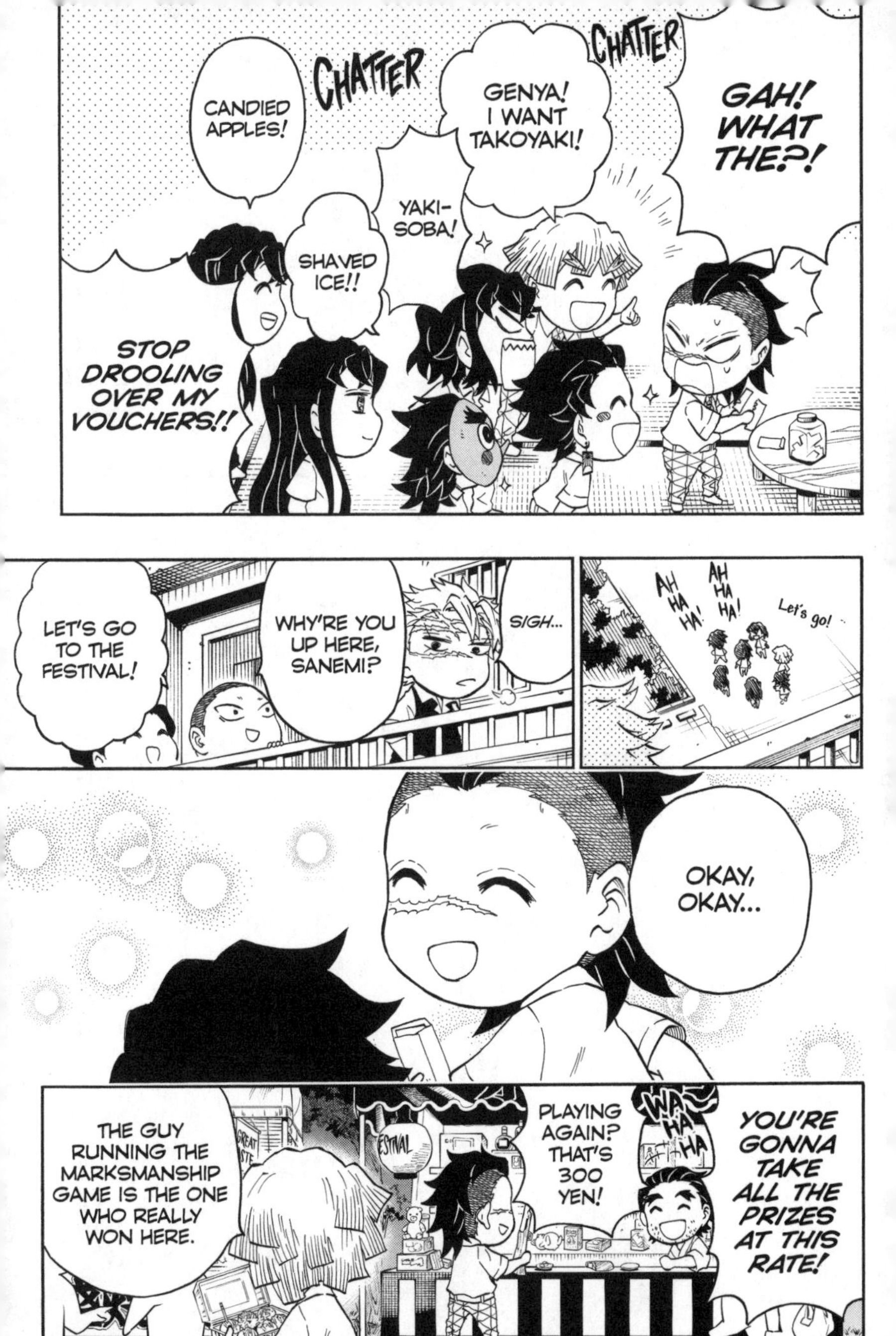
CHATTER
GAH! WHAT THE?!
GENYA! I WANT TAKOYAKI!
CHATTER
YAKI-SOBA!
CANDIED APPLES!
SHAVED ICE!!
STOP DROOLING OVER MY VOUCHERS!!
AH HA HA!
AH HA HA!
Let's go!
SIGH...
WHY'RE YOU UP HERE, SANEMI?
LET'S GO TO THE FESTIVAL!
OKAY, OKAY...
YOU'RE GONNA TAKE ALL THE PRIZES AT THIS RATE!
WA HA HA
PLAYING AGAIN? THAT'S 300 YEN!
FESTIVAL
THE GUY RUNNING THE MARKSMANSHIP GAME IS THE ONE WHO REALLY WON HERE.

TOKITOS

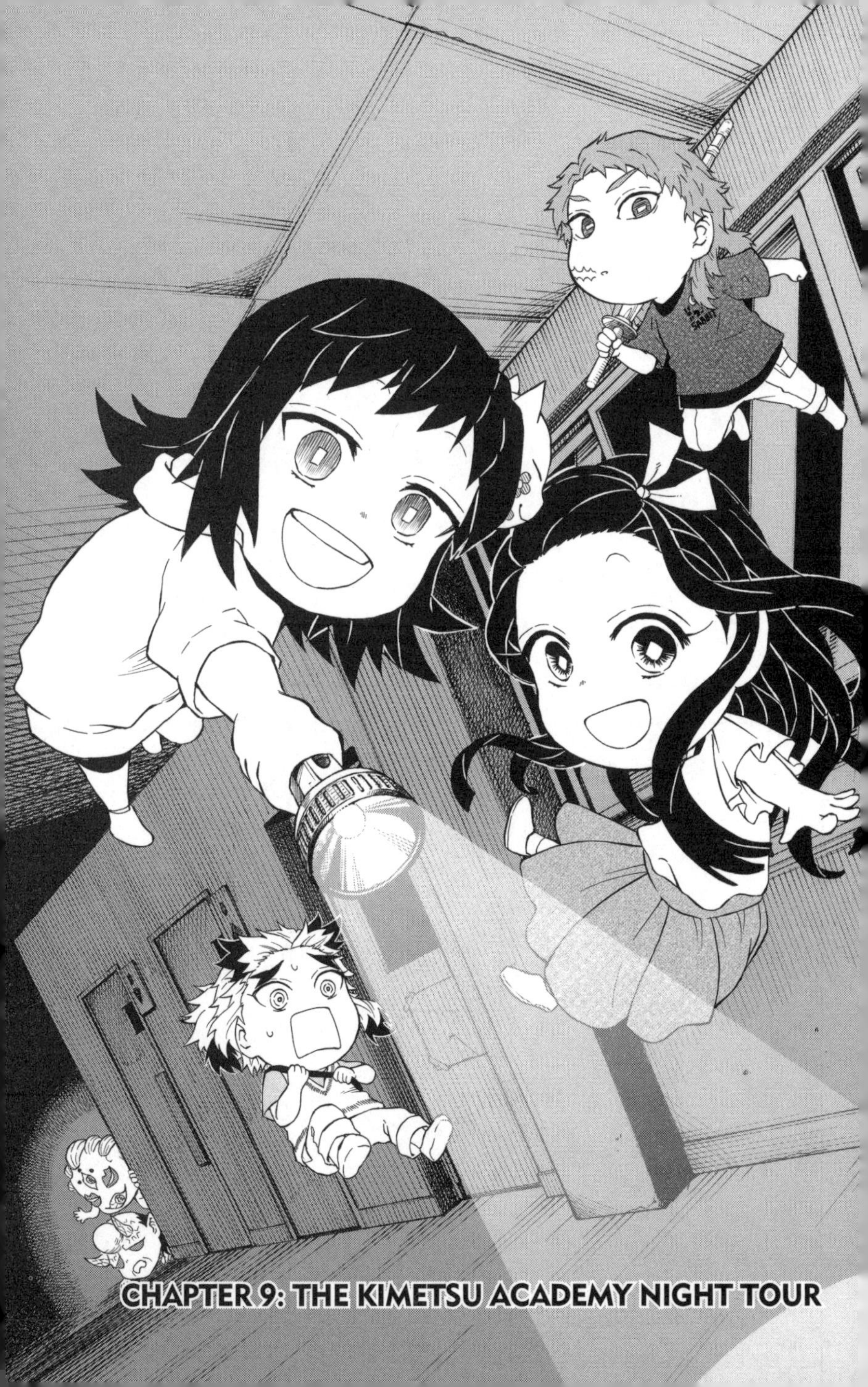

CHAPTER 9: THE KIMETSU ACADEMY NIGHT TOUR

IDEAS FOR THE SCHOOL'S SEVEN MYSTERIES?

YEAH! THE SCHOOL PAPER...

...PUT OUT A CALL FOR IDEAS!

Cool!

"ONCE WE HAVE SEVEN, WE'LL ANNOUNCE THE CHOSEN MYSTERIES."

SPOOKY STORIES, HUH?

"...SO WE'RE LOOKING FOR YOUR SPOOKY STORIES."

"LIKE OTHER SCHOOLS, KIMETSU ACADEMY SHOULD HAVE SEVEN MYSTERIOUS HAUNTINGS ..."

IT SAYS, UM...

LET'S VISIT THE SCHOOL AT NIGHT TO GET IDEAS!!

THE JUNIOR HIGH...

TARO CLASS
SECOND-YEAR

MAKOMO
TARO CLASS
JUNIOR HIGH, SECOND-YEAR

NEZUKO KAMADO
TARO CLASS
JUNIOR HIGH, SECOND-YEAR

IDEAS FOR WHAT?

...FOR A GHOST-HUNTING ADVENTURE!

SO WE'LL SNEAK INTO SCHOOL AT NIGHT...

WE NEED A GOOD STORY TO SUBMIT!

DIDN'T YOU SEE THE SCHOOL PAPER?

WHAT ARE YOU TALKING ABOUT?

THAT'S WHY WE'LL KEEP IT A SECRET!

THERE'S NO WAY THE TEACHERS OR OUR PARENTS WOULD LET US!

WAIT, WE CAN'T!

ADVENTURE...

YAY

HMM

TELL YOUR PARENTS YOU'RE SLEEPING OVER AT MY HOUSE!

BRING A FLASHLIGHT AND JUNK FOOD!

...

SABITO
TARO CLASS
JUNIOR HIGH,
SECOND-YEAR

WILL IT BE DANGEROUS?

COULD BE!

THAT'S WHY WE'LL NEED A BODY-GUARD!

YAY! NOW WE'LL BE SAFE!!

WOO HOO

YAHOO!!

WELL, I GUESS I COULD...

BODY-GUARD

NEZUKO AGREED TO GO.

HM?

...EXCUSE ME?

UM...

YOU CAN INVITE A FRIEND IF YOU WANT!

DON'T BE A SPOIL-SPORT!

BUT ISN'T THIS A BIT KIDDY FOR JUNIOR HIGH?

...AND THIS CLASS WRITTEN ON IT.

I FOUND THIS, AND IT HAD YOUR NAME...

SENJURO RENGOKU
AUTUMN LEAVES CLASS
JUNIOR HIGH, FIRST-YEAR

OH!

WAIT, SENJURO!

YES?

NO PROBLEM!

WELL, I'LL BE GOING NOW!

OH! MY HAND-KERCHIEF!

THANK YOU, SENJURO!

THAT NIGHT...

...AT THE JUNIOR HIGH...

WHOA...

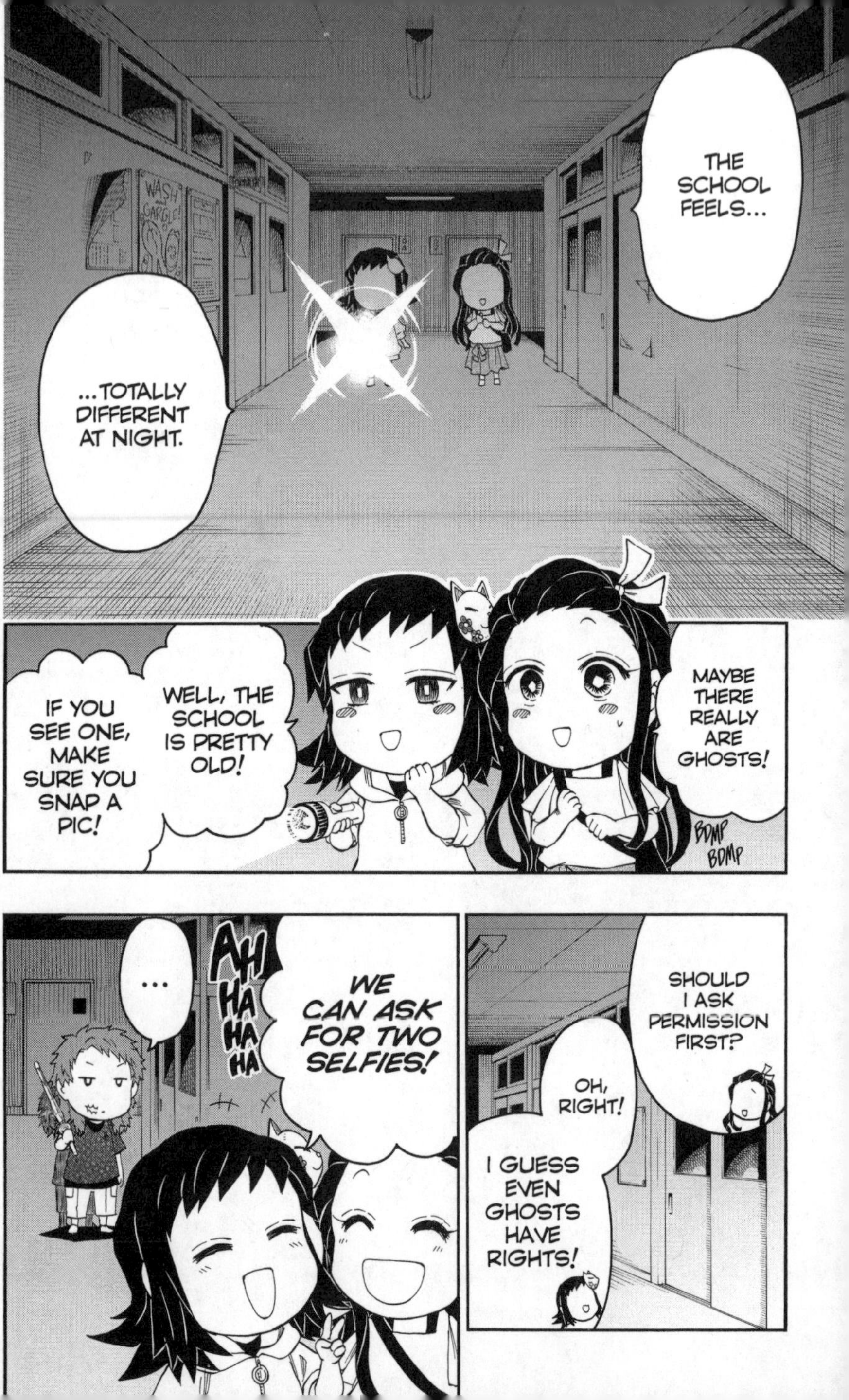
THE SCHOOL FEELS...
...TOTALLY DIFFERENT AT NIGHT.
MAYBE THERE REALLY ARE GHOSTS!
BDMP BDMP
WELL, THE SCHOOL IS PRETTY OLD!
IF YOU SEE ONE, MAKE SURE YOU SNAP A PIC!
SHOULD I ASK PERMISSION FIRST?
OH, RIGHT!
I GUESS EVEN GHOSTS HAVE RIGHTS!
WE CAN ASK FOR TWO SELFIES!
AHHAHAHA
...

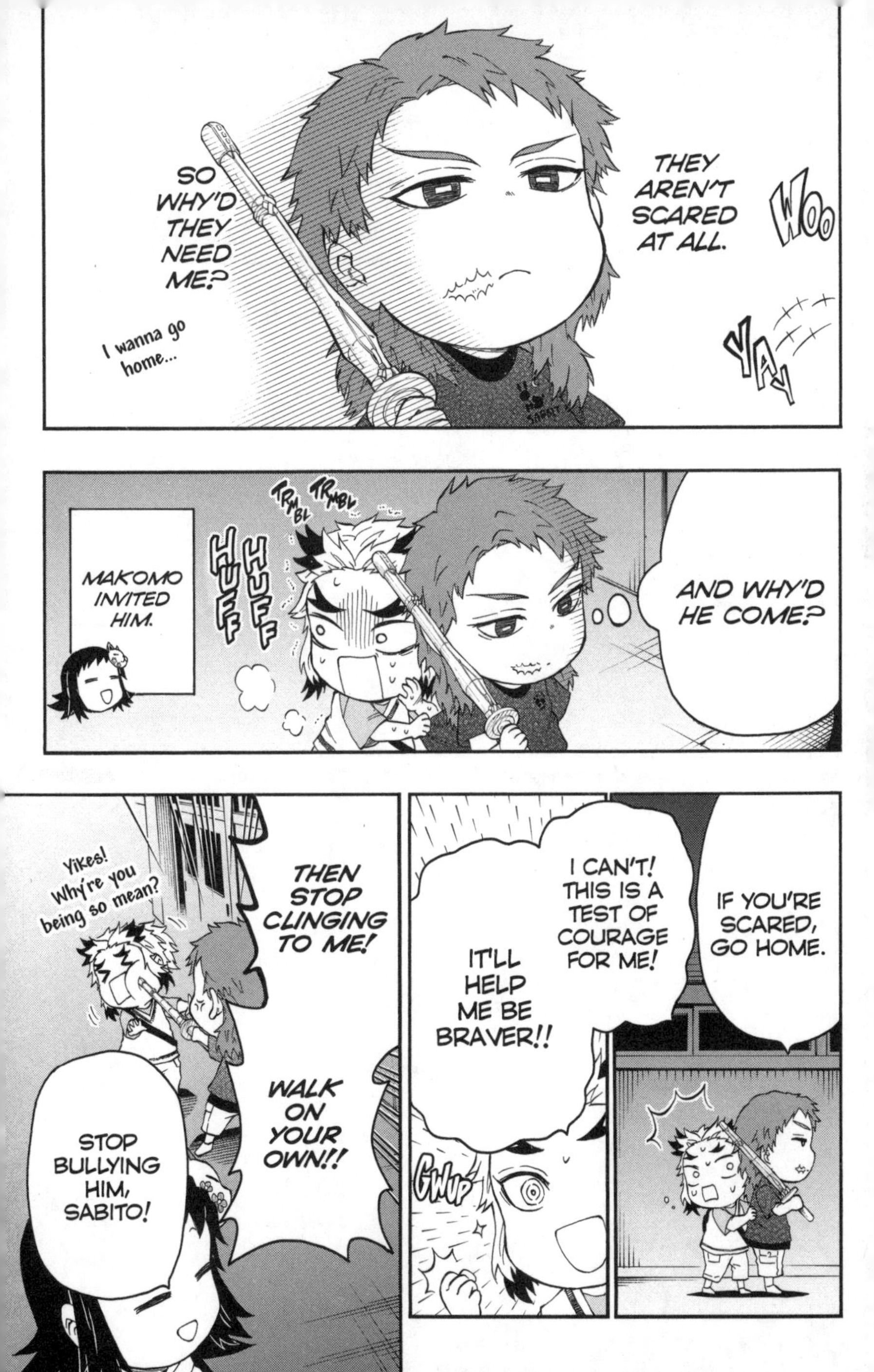
WOO
YAY
THEY AREN'T SCARED AT ALL.
SO WHY'D THEY NEED ME?
I wanna go home...
AND WHY'D HE COME?
TRMBL TRMBL
HUFF HUFF
MAKOMO INVITED HIM.
IF YOU'RE SCARED, GO HOME.
I CAN'T! THIS IS A TEST OF COURAGE FOR ME!
IT'LL HELP ME BE BRAVER!!
GWUP
THEN STOP CLINGING TO ME!
Yikes! Why're you being so mean?
WALK ON YOUR OWN!!
STOP BULLYING HIM, SABITO!

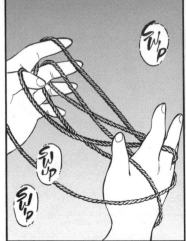

SHH!

!

MAYBE THE SCIENCE ROOM?

SO! WHERE SHOULD WE LOOK?

LOOK!

WHAT'S WRONG, SABITO?

SOME- ONE'S IN THE CLASS- ROOM!

TH- THEN IS THAT...

...A G-G- GHOST?

NO ONE ELSE SHOULD BE HERE THIS LATE!

AH!

WHERE?

WHAT ?!

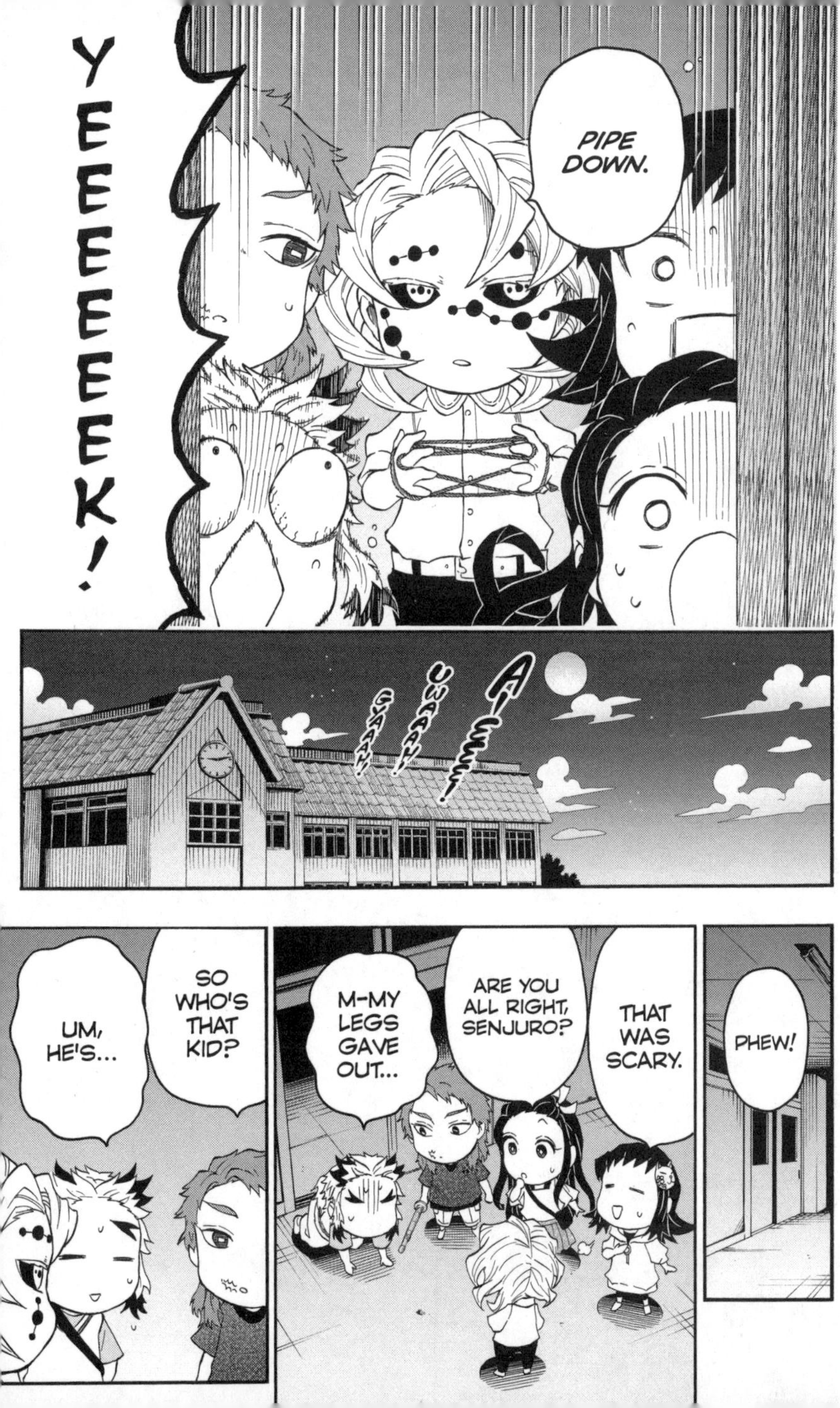
PIPE DOWN.
YEEEEEEK!
AIEEEE!
UWAAAAH!
GYAAAAH!
PHEW!
THAT WAS SCARY.
ARE YOU ALL RIGHT, SENJURO?
M-MY LEGS GAVE OUT...
SO WHO'S THAT KID?
UM, HE'S...

SORRY. THEY'RE ALL IDIOTS.

...

CAN YOU MAKE TOKYO TOWER?!

YOU DON'T NEED TO BE SO GRUMPY.

OOH, *ATTITUDE* MUCH?

...TRY THE HIGH SCHOOL.

IF YOU WANT SPOOKS...

NO IDEA.

CAN YOU S-SENSE SPIRITS?

TMP TMP

SERIOUSLY?

THERE'S A WEIRD FEELING IN THE AIR.

HUH? WHY?

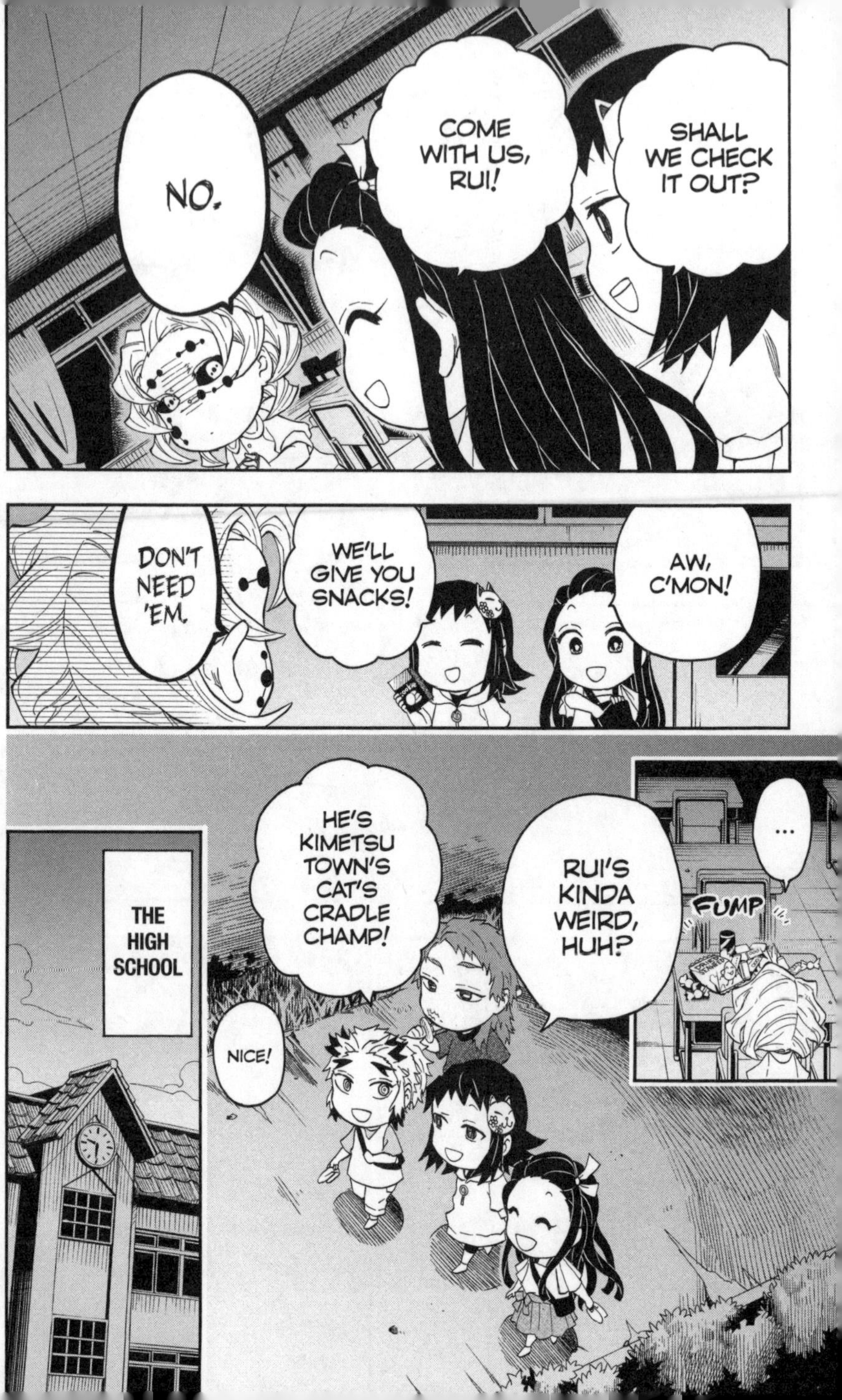
SHALL WE CHECK IT OUT?
COME WITH US, RUI!
NO.
AW, C'MON!
WE'LL GIVE YOU SNACKS!
DON'T NEED 'EM.
...
FUMP
RUI'S KINDA WEIRD, HUH?
HE'S KIMETSU TOWN'S CAT'S CRADLE CHAMP!
NICE!
THE HIGH SCHOOL

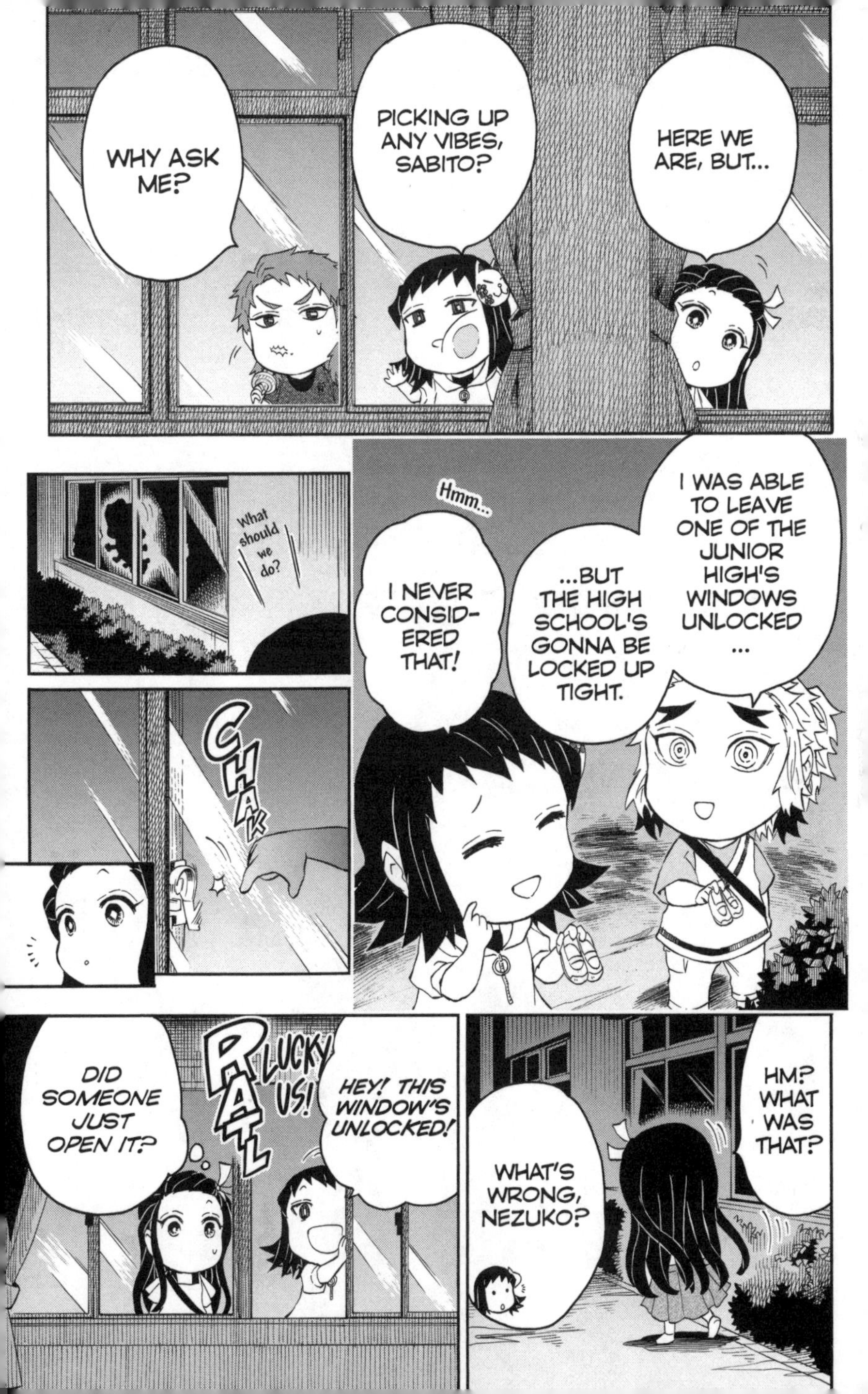
HERE WE ARE, BUT...
PICKING UP ANY VIBES, SABITO?
WHY ASK ME?
I WAS ABLE TO LEAVE ONE OF THE JUNIOR HIGH'S WINDOWS UNLOCKED ...
...BUT THE HIGH SCHOOL'S GONNA BE LOCKED UP TIGHT.
Hmm...
I NEVER CONSID-ERED THAT!
What should we do?
CHAK
HM? WHAT WAS THAT?
WHAT'S WRONG, NEZUKO?
HEY! THIS WINDOW'S UNLOCKED!
LUCKY US!
RATTL
DID SOMEONE JUST OPEN IT?

YEAH. THAT'S THE ACTUAL SCARY THING HERE.

...TO WORRY ABOUT WHETHER WE COULD GET IN TROUBLE FOR THIS?

IS IT TOO LATE...

RELAX!

LET'S START WITH THE THIRD FLOOR...

...AND WORK OUR WAY DOWN.

PSHOOO

DID YOU HEAR THAT?

YEAH, LIKE WEIRD BREATHING...

IT'S KINDA CREEPY.

PSHH

SHIVR

PSHHHH

PWUF

PWUF

PSHOOO

PSHH

ANYWAY, THERE MUST BE SOMETHING HERE! RUI SAID SO!

HM?

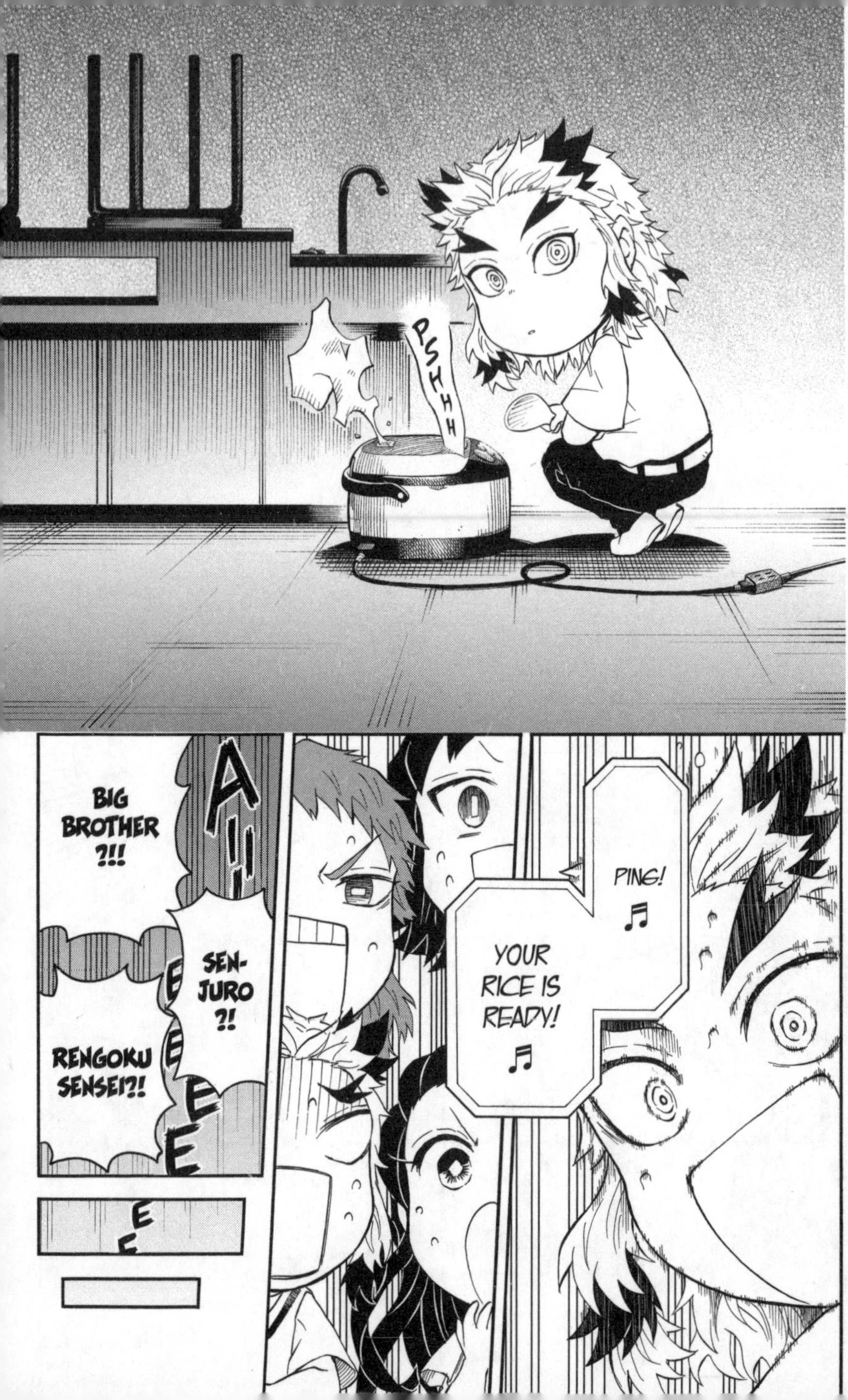
PSHHH
PING! ♫
YOUR RICE IS READY! ♫
AIIEEEEE
BIG BROTHER?!!
SEN-JURO?!
RENGOKU SENSEI?!
EE

OH DEAR...

KYOJURO RENGOKU
HISTORY TEACHER
(SENJURO'S OLDER BROTHER)

YOU'RE HERE TOO, BIG BRO...

IS HE GONNA LECTURE US?!

WHAT ARE YOU DOING HERE AT THIS HOUR?!

...who reaps rice in the home ec room!

The steamy specter...

CAN I TAKE A PIC FOR THE SCHOOL PAPER?

PLEASE DON'T, YOUNG MAN!

YEP!! I'VE GOT THE MUNCHIES!

HERE FOR A LATE-NIGHT SNACK?

BUT WHY SNACK AT SCHOOL?

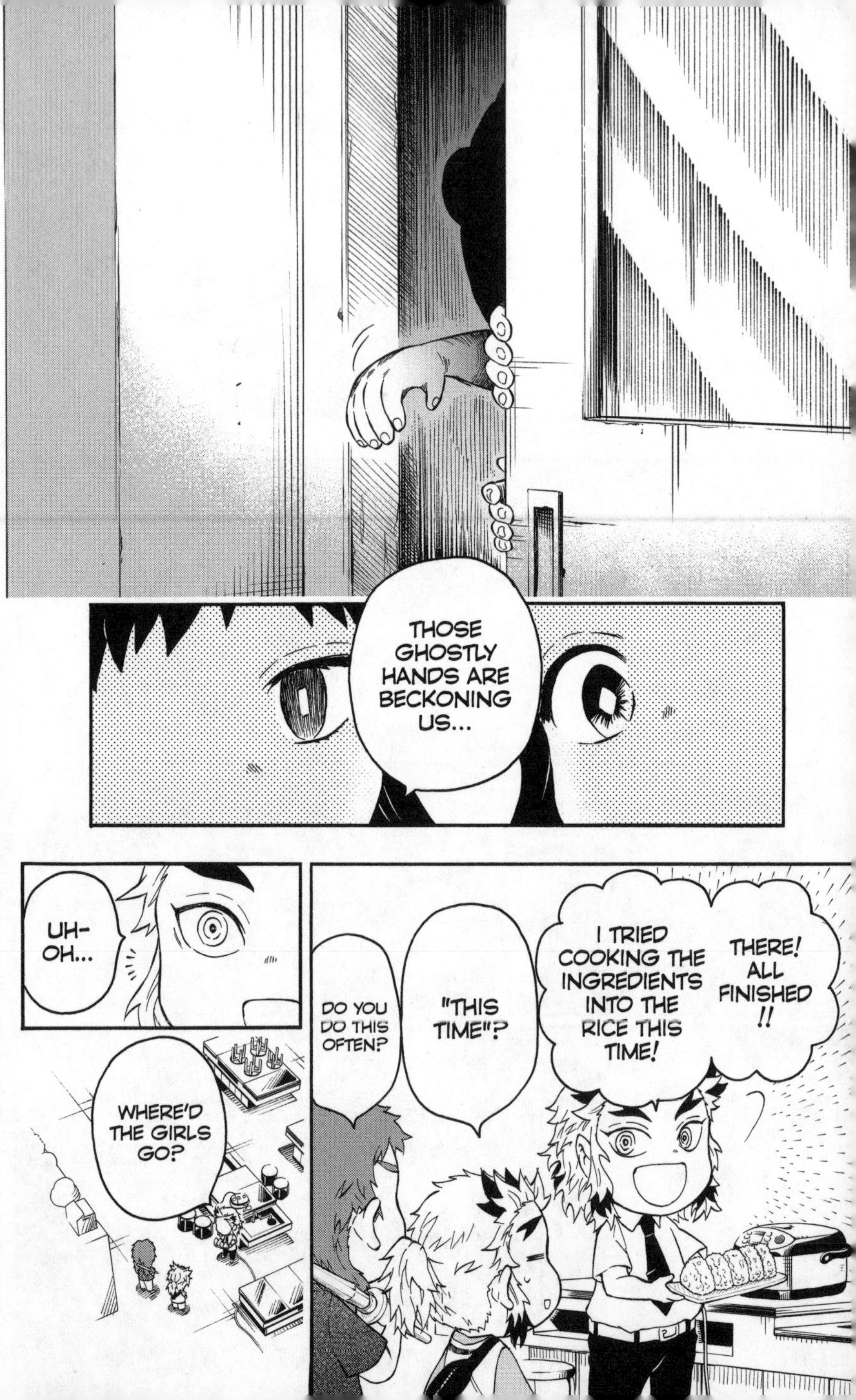
THOSE GHOSTLY HANDS ARE BECKONING US...
THERE! ALL FINISHED!!
I TRIED COOKING THE INGREDIENTS INTO THE RICE THIS TIME!
"THIS TIME"?
DO YOU DO THIS OFTEN?
UH-OH...
WHERE'D THE GIRLS GO?

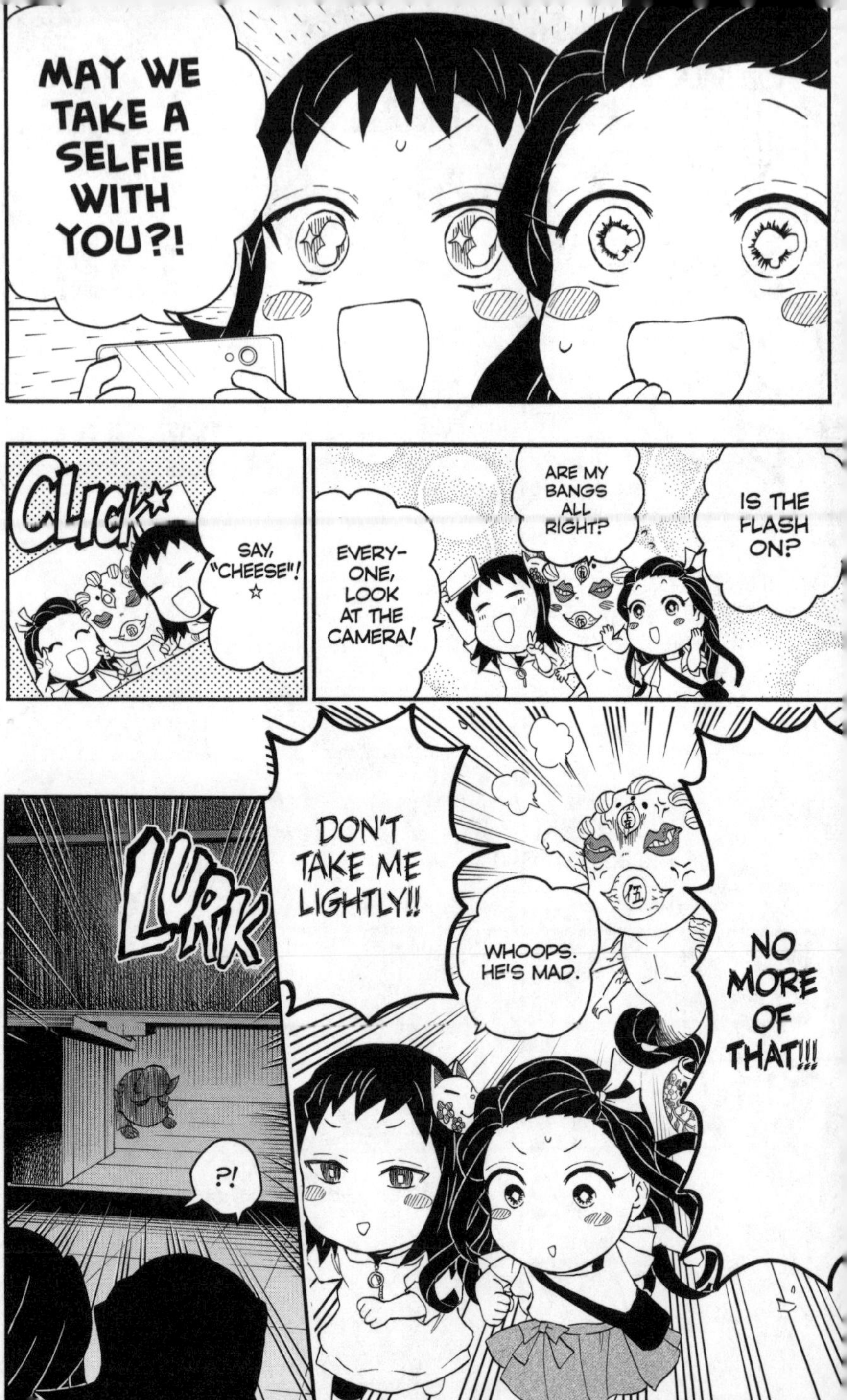
MAY WE TAKE A SELFIE WITH YOU?!
IS THE FLASH ON?
ARE MY BANGS ALL RIGHT?
EVERY-ONE, LOOK AT THE CAMERA!
SAY, "CHEESE"! ☆
CLICK☆
NO MORE OF THAT!!!
DON'T TAKE ME LIGHTLY!!
WHOOPS. HE'S MAD.
LURK
?!

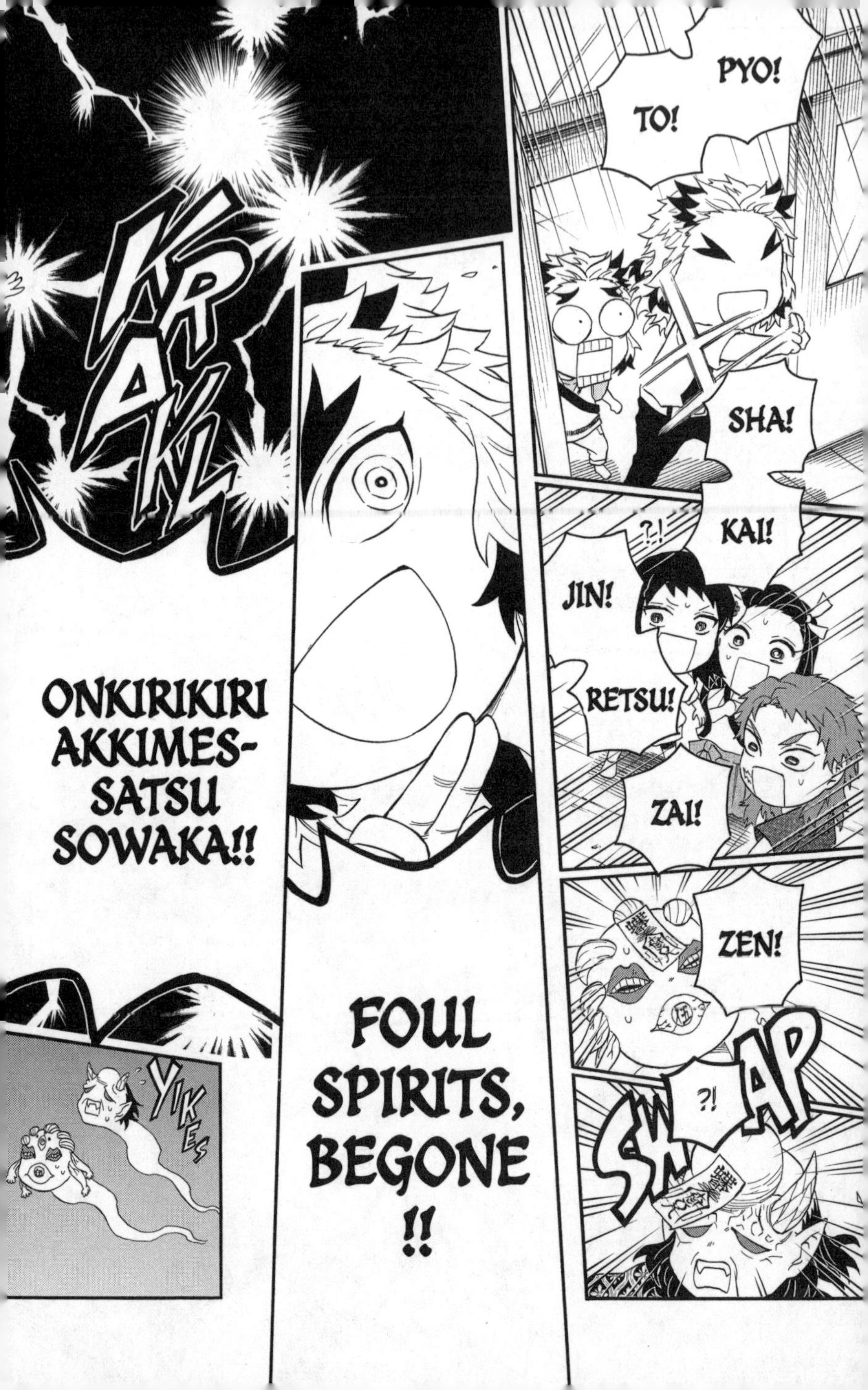
PYO!
TO!
SHA!
KAI!
?!
JIN!
RETSU!
ZAI!
ZEN!
?!
SNAP
FOUL SPIRITS, BEGONE !!
ONKIRIKIRI AKKIMES- SATSU SOWAKA!!
YIKES

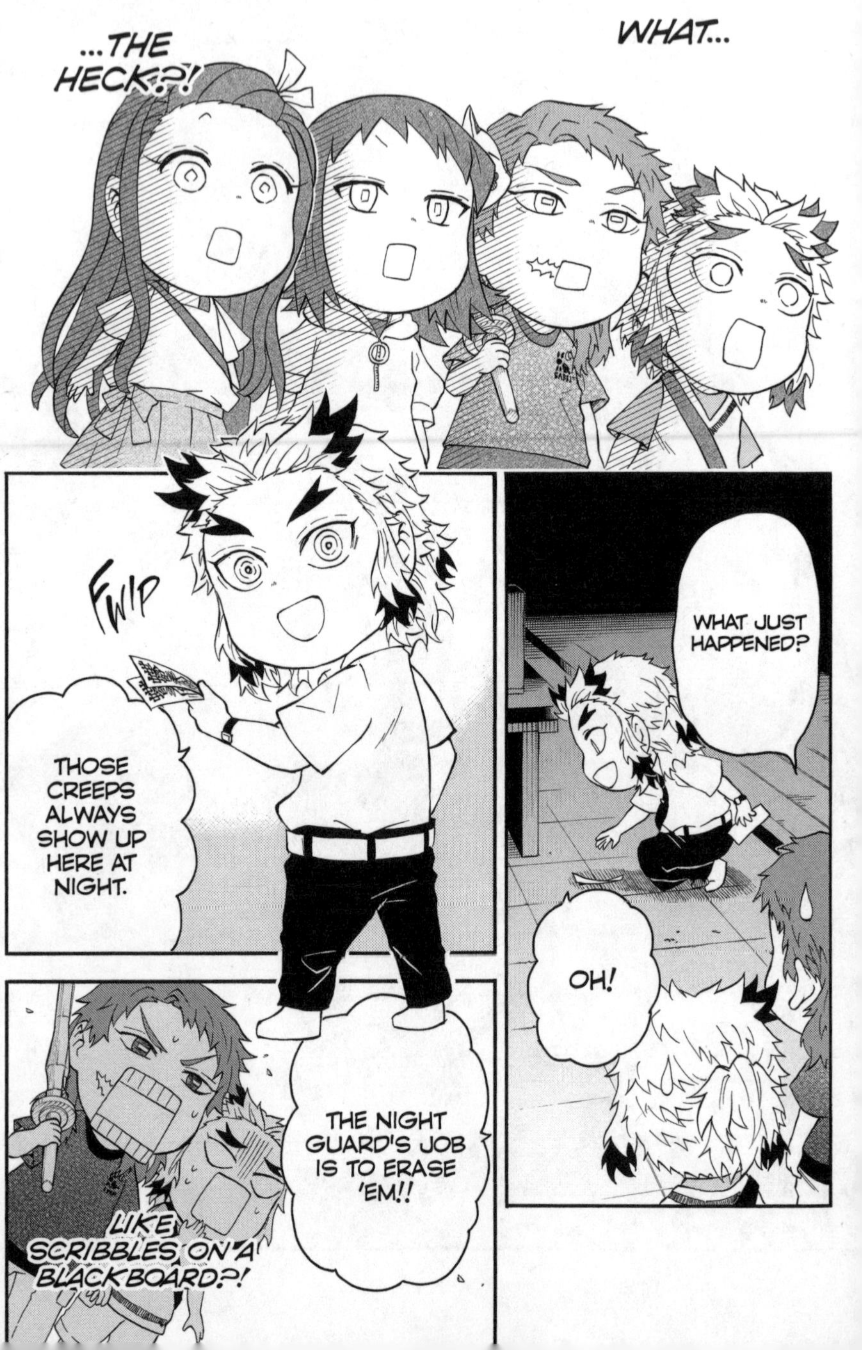
WHAT...
...THE HECK?!
WHAT JUST HAPPENED?
OH!
FWIP
THOSE CREEPS ALWAYS SHOW UP HERE AT NIGHT.
THE NIGHT GUARD'S JOB IS TO ERASE 'EM!!
LIKE SCRIBBLES ON A BLACKBOARD?!

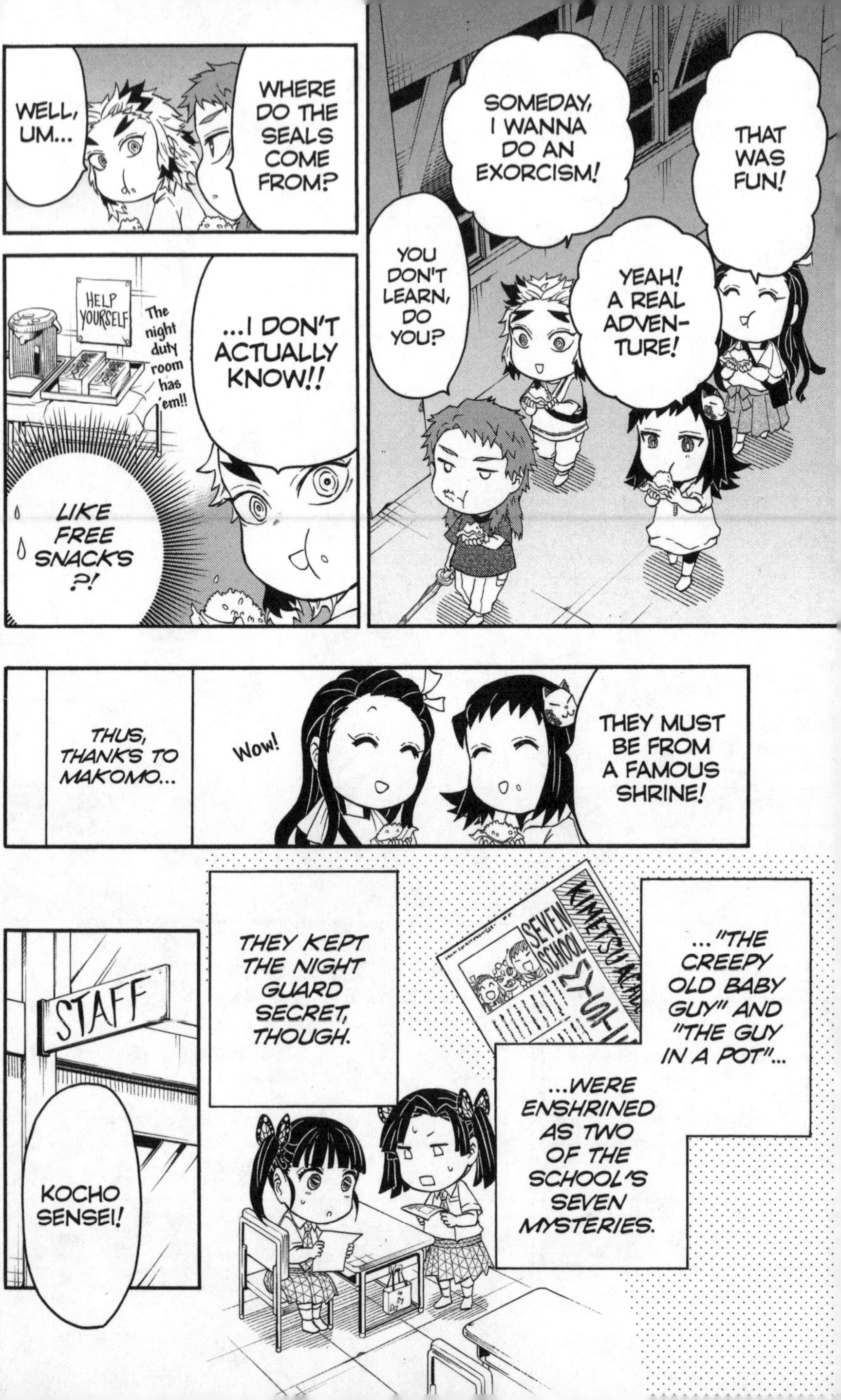
THAT WAS FUN!
SOMEDAY, I WANNA DO AN EXORCISM!
YEAH! A REAL ADVENTURE!
YOU DON'T LEARN, DO YOU?
WHERE DO THE SEALS COME FROM?
WELL, UM...
...I DON'T ACTUALLY KNOW!!
The night duty room has 'em!!
HELP YOURSELF
LIKE FREE SNACKS?!
THEY MUST BE FROM A FAMOUS SHRINE!
Wow!
THUS, THANKS TO MAKOMO...
..."THE CREEPY OLD BABY GUY" AND "THE GUY IN A POT"...
...WERE ENSHRINED AS TWO OF THE SCHOOL'S SEVEN MYSTERIES.
SEVEN
SCHOOL
THEY KEPT THE NIGHT GUARD SECRET, THOUGH.
STAFF
KOCHO SENSEI!

LIFE IN TARO CLASS

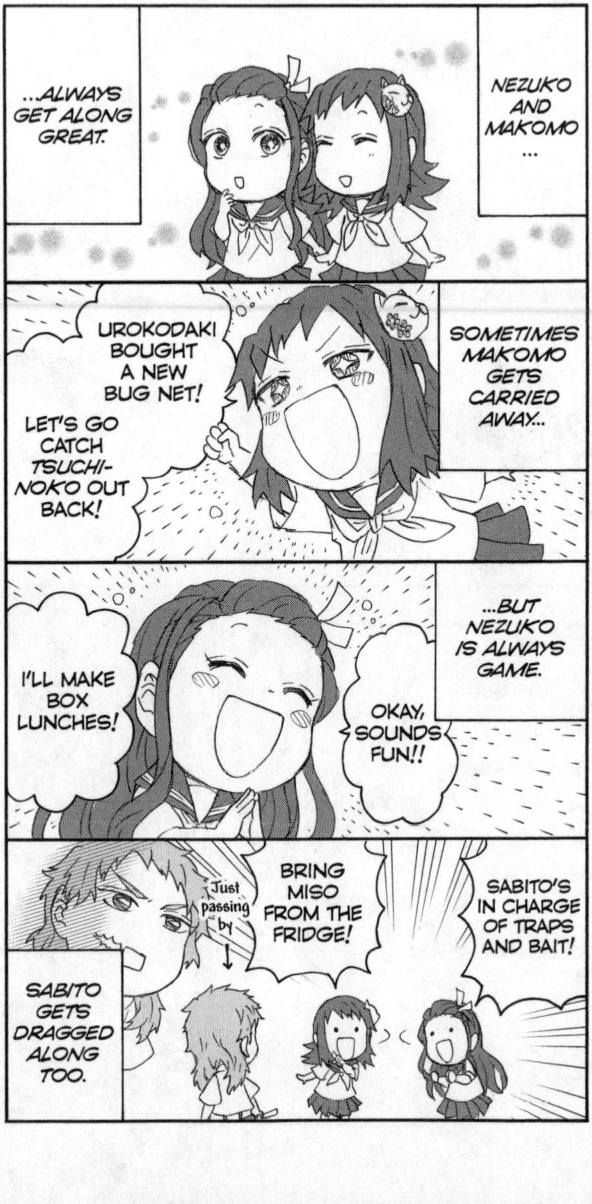
NEZUKO AND MAKOMO ...
...ALWAYS GET ALONG GREAT.
SOMETIMES MAKOMO GETS CARRIED AWAY...
UROKODAKI BOUGHT A NEW BUG NET!
LET'S GO CATCH TSUCHI-NOKO OUT BACK!
...BUT NEZUKO IS ALWAYS GAME.
OKAY, SOUNDS FUN!!
I'LL MAKE BOX LUNCHES!
SABITO'S IN CHARGE OF TRAPS AND BAIT!
BRING MISO FROM THE FRIDGE!
Just passing by
SABITO GETS DRAGGED ALONG TOO.

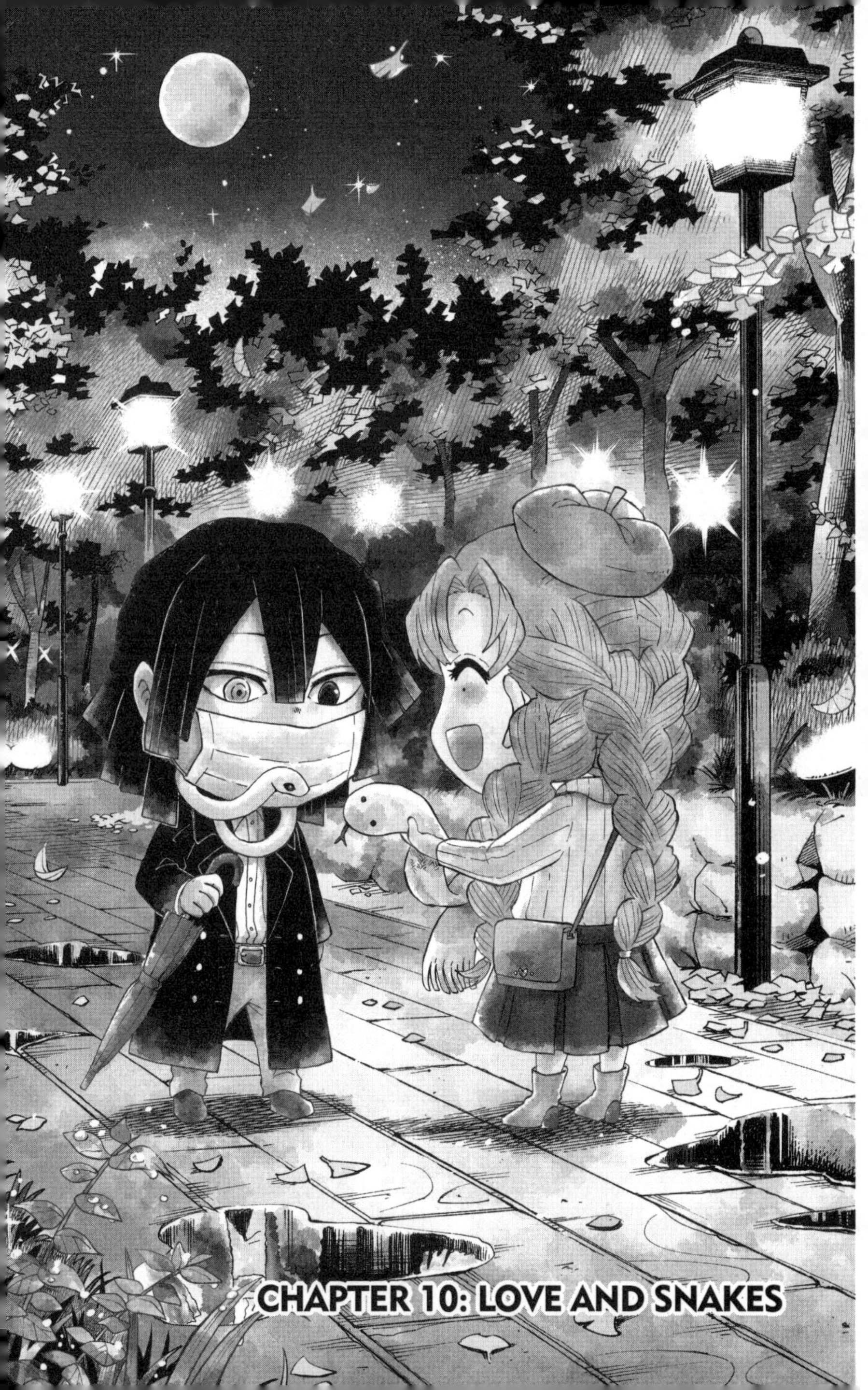
CHAPTER 10: LOVE AND SNAKES

NO FREAKING WAY...

IT'S FOR...

CHEMISTRY

...OBANAI IGURO?! OUR CHEMISTRY TEACHER?!

WAG WAG

Oh, you forgot your homework?

NOT A CHANCE!

WELL, I GUESS HE'S POPULAR!

HE'S A GLOOMY AND ANNOYING SNAKE!!

Then why even bother coming?!

ROMANCE ISN'T A COMPETITION! BE STRONG, ZENITSU!

HE BEAT ME!!

I CAN'T BELIEVE IT!!

FINE, WHATEVER. BUT...

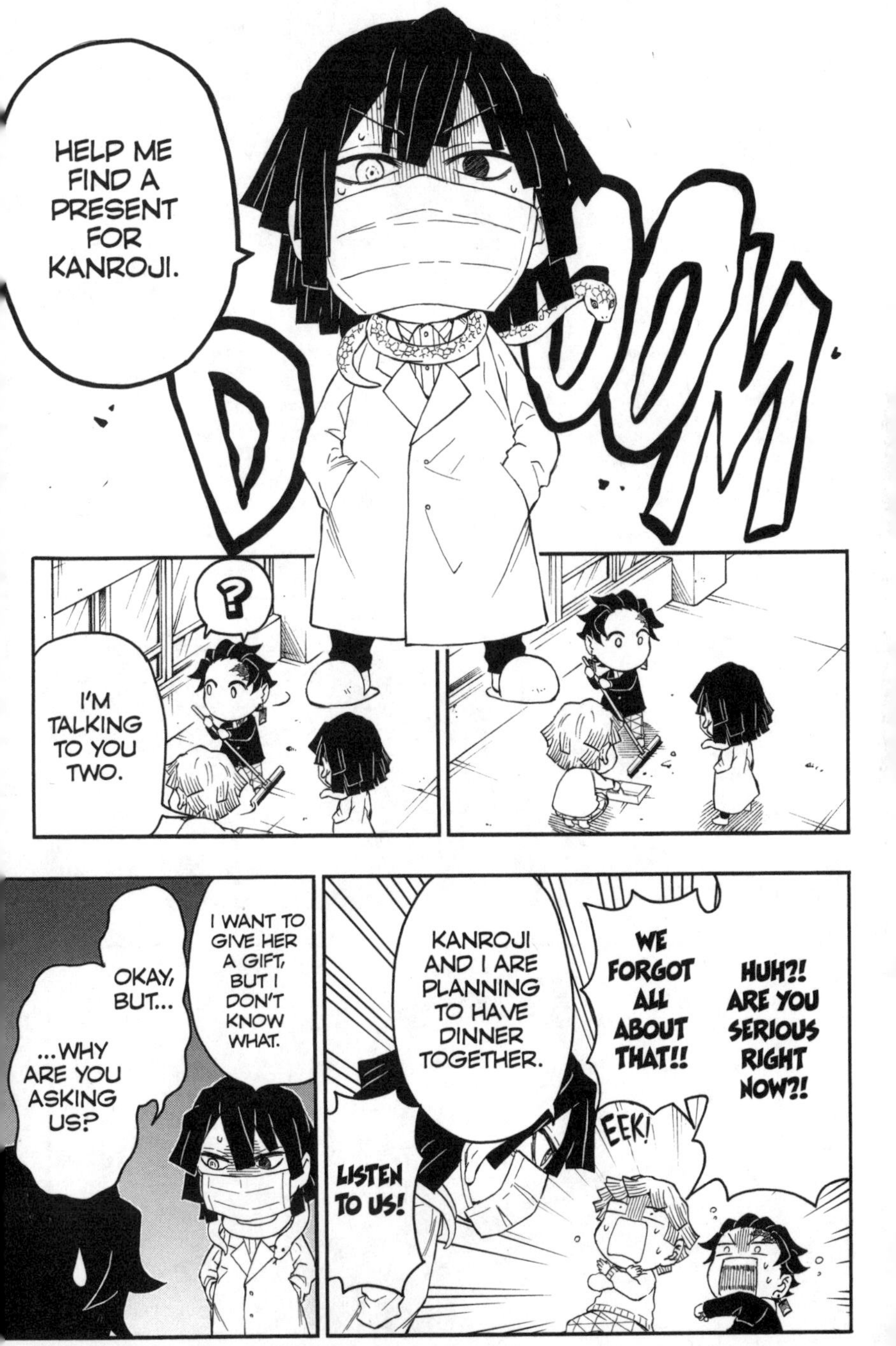
HELP ME FIND A PRESENT FOR KANROJI.
?
I'M TALKING TO YOU TWO.
I WANT TO GIVE HER A GIFT, BUT I DON'T KNOW WHAT.
OKAY, BUT...
...WHY ARE YOU ASKING US?
KANROJI AND I ARE PLANNING TO HAVE DINNER TOGETHER.
WE FORGOT ALL ABOUT THAT!!
HUH?! ARE YOU SERIOUS RIGHT NOW?!
EEK!
LISTEN TO US!

KANROJI WENT TO SCHOOL HERE, RIGHT?

I WOULD RATHER NOT INVOLVE STUDENTS BUT...

EVERYONE WHO KNOWS HER RECOMMENDED FOOD.

WHY NOT ASK THE OTHER TEACHERS?

...YOU'RE THE ONLY ONES I CAN TRUST WHO KNOW ABOUT THIS.

*IGURO DIDN'T START WORKING HERE UNTIL AFTER SHE GRADUATED.

WE ALWAYS GO OUT TO EAT, SO I NEED SOMETHING BESIDES FOOD!

WHAT'S WITH THE LOOK?

DOES HE...NOT HAVE ANY NON-WORK FRIENDS HE COULD ASK?

SURE! I'D BE HAPPY TO!!

WHAT?!

WHY SHOULD I CARE...

...ABOUT SOME OTHER GUY'S DATE GOING WELL?

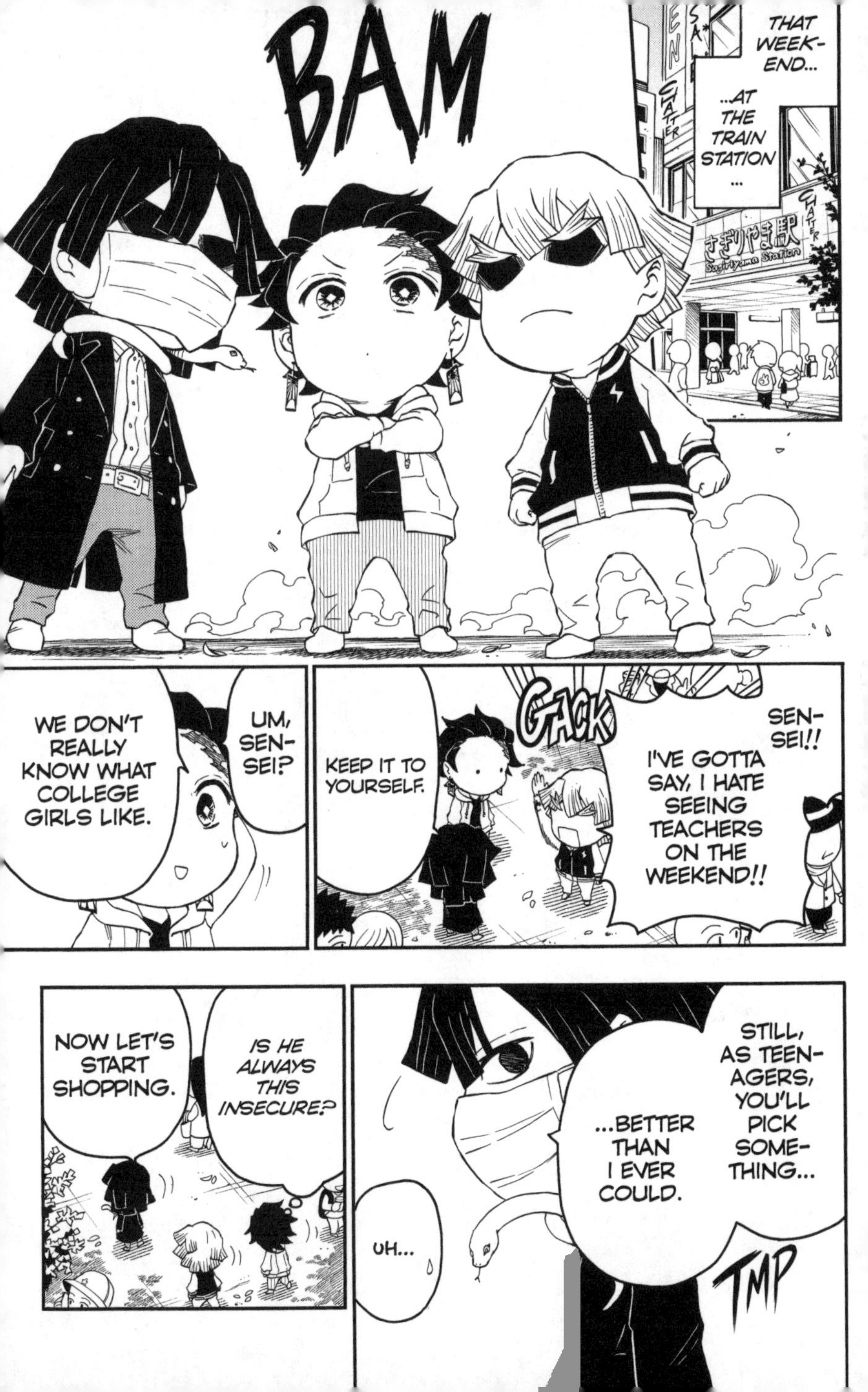
THAT WEEK-END...
...AT THE TRAIN STATION...
CHATTER
さぎりやま駅
Sagiriyama Station
CHATTER
BAM
GACK
SEN-SEI!!
I'VE GOTTA SAY, I HATE SEEING TEACHERS ON THE WEEKEND!!
KEEP IT TO YOURSELF.
UM, SEN-SEI?
WE DON'T REALLY KNOW WHAT COLLEGE GIRLS LIKE.
STILL, AS TEEN-AGERS, YOU'LL PICK SOME-THING...
...BETTER THAN I EVER COULD.
UH...
TMP
IS HE ALWAYS THIS INSECURE?
NOW LET'S START SHOPPING.

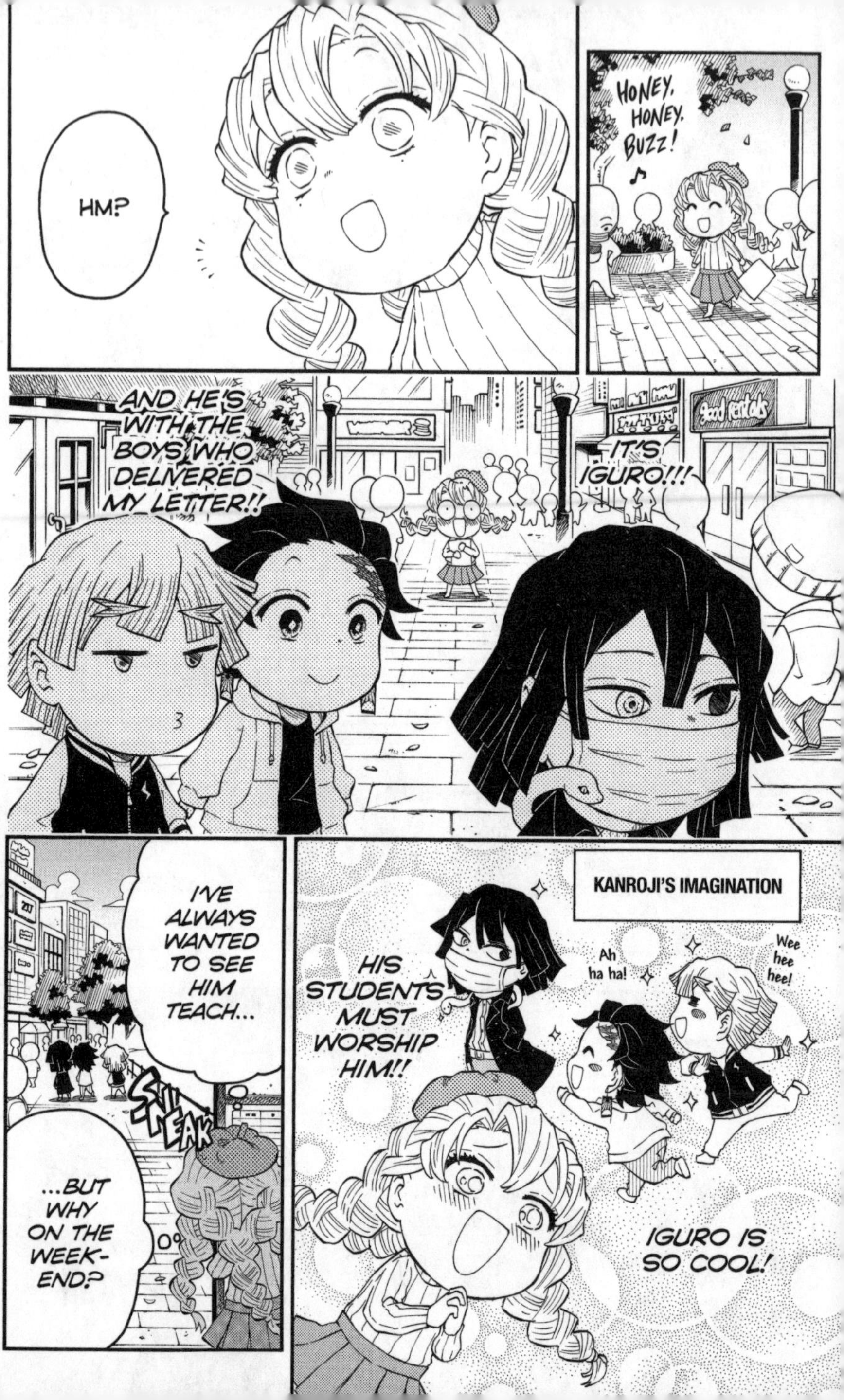
HONEY, HONEY. BUZZ! ♪
HM?
IT'S IGURO!!!
AND HE'S WITH THE BOYS WHO DELIVERED MY LETTER!!
good rentals
KANROJI'S IMAGINATION
Wee hee hee!
Ah ha ha!
HIS STUDENTS MUST WORSHIP HIM!!
IGURO IS SO COOL!
I'VE ALWAYS WANTED TO SEE HIM TEACH...
SNEAK
...BUT WHY ON THE WEEK-END?

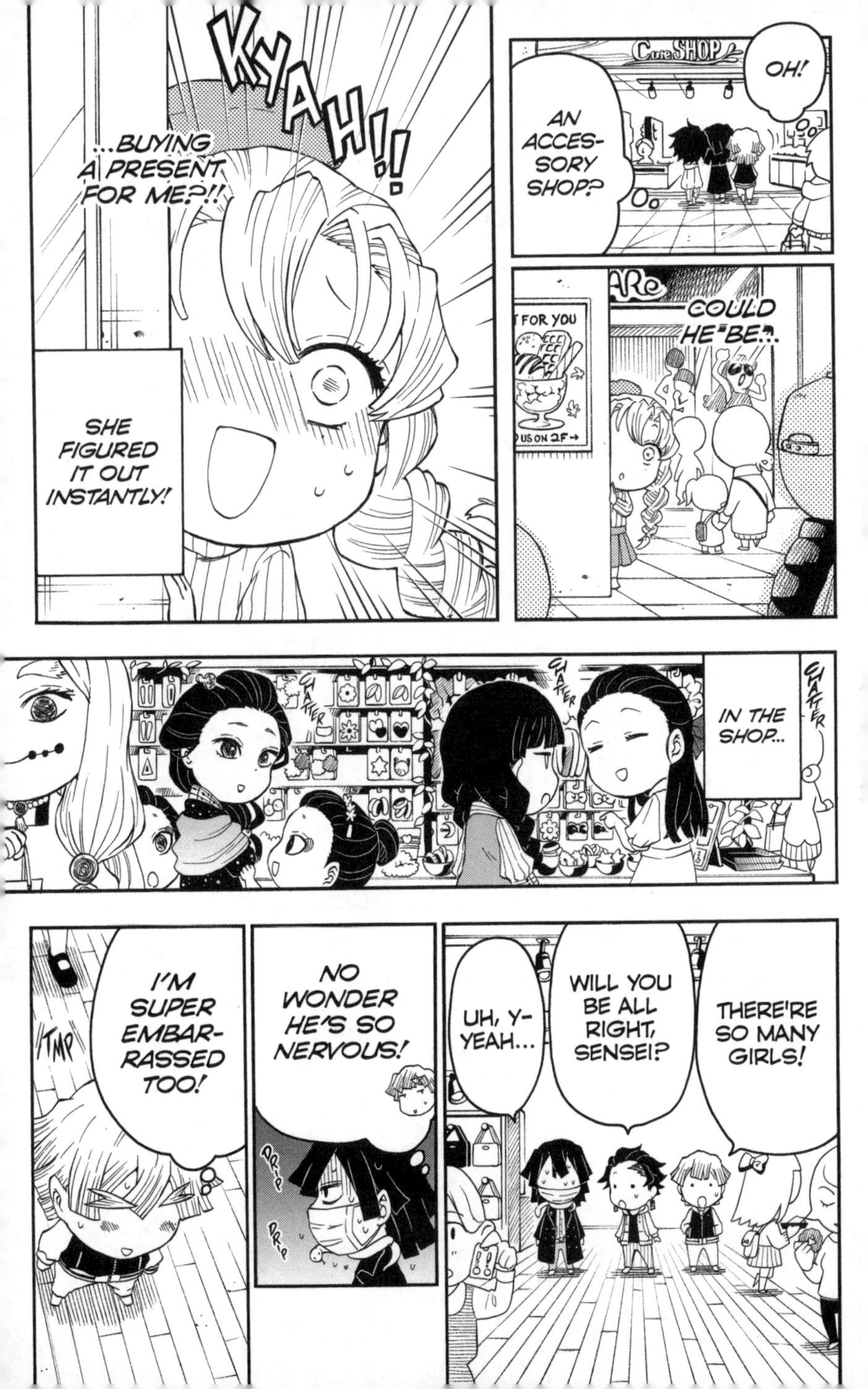

Cute SHOP
OH!
AN ACCES-SORY SHOP?
FOR YOU
COULD HE BE...?
KYAH!!
...BUYING A PRESENT FOR ME?!!
SHE FIGURED IT OUT INSTANTLY!
CHATTER
IN THE SHOP...
CHATTER
CHATTER
THERE'RE SO MANY GIRLS!
WILL YOU BE ALL RIGHT, SENSEI?
UH, Y-YEAH...
NO WONDER HE'S SO NERVOUS!
DRIP
DRIP
I'M SUPER EMBAR-RASSED TOO!
TMP

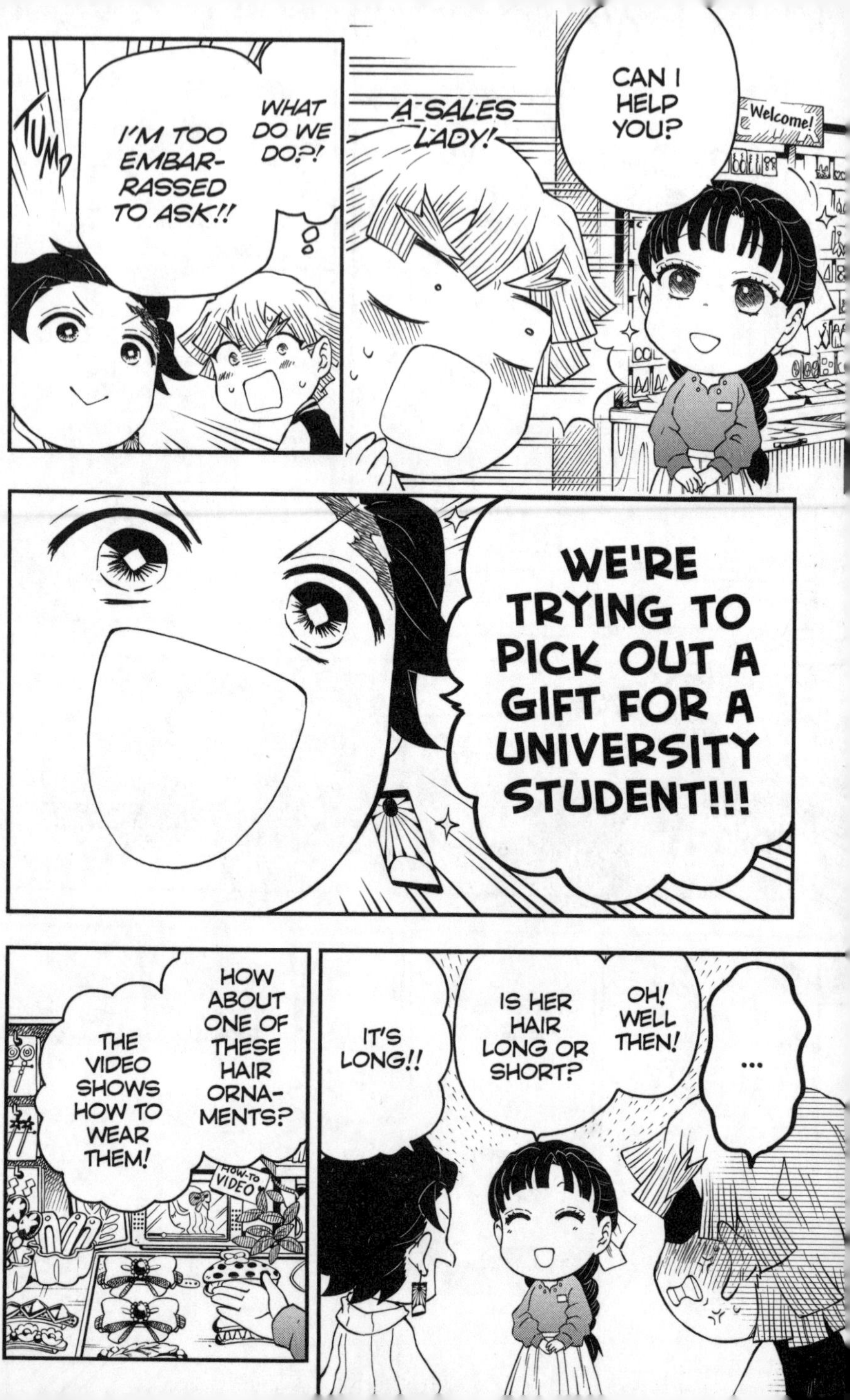
Welcome!
CAN I HELP YOU?
A SALES LADY!
WHAT DO WE DO?!
I'M TOO EMBARRASSED TO ASK!!
TUMP
WE'RE TRYING TO PICK OUT A GIFT FOR A UNIVERSITY STUDENT!!!
...
OH! WELL THEN!
IS HER HAIR LONG OR SHORT?
IT'S LONG!!
HOW ABOUT ONE OF THESE HAIR ORNAMENTS?
THE VIDEO SHOWS HOW TO WEAR THEM!
HOW-TO VIDEO

GUH!

BOOM

WE'RE HERE BECAUSE OF YOU!!

YOU'RE PRETENDING WE'RE STRANGERS?!!

HOWEVER...

THAT SETTLES IT! NOW—

HOW ABOUT A HAIR ORNAMENT, SENSEI?

HMM...

I BET THIS ONE'D LOOK GOOD ON KANROJI.

SHE'LL BE WEARING IT AROUND OTHER PEOPLE, SO IT'S MORE IMPORTANT...

...WHETHER IT'S TO HER TASTE.

I WOULDN'T WANT HER TO FEEL OBLIGATED TO WEAR SOMETHING SHE DIDN'T LIKE.

YES, IT WOULD...

GWOOOOOOO

THE ROAD AHEAD LOOKED LONG.

...

STMP

I'LL THINK ABOUT IT.

ON TO ANOTHER SHOP.

IT'S PAST NOON.

Nope...

No...

Not this one...

Not this one either...

IF HE ASKED FOR OUR HELP...

...HE MUST BE SERIOUS ABOUT THIS.

IS SHOPPING FOR GIRLS REALLY THAT HARD?

What a pain!

WE HAVEN'T MADE ANY PROGRESS ALL MORNING!

ARE YOU EVEN TRYING?!

SHALL WE BREAK FOR LUNCH?

I'LL DECIDE THIS AFTERNOON.

FAMILY RESTAURANT

Welcome!

HONESTLY, I PREFER FINER DINING...

DOES THIS PLACE WORK FOR YOU?

YEAH! THE MENU'S GOT VARIETY!

WHOA

LET'S DIG IN!!

MNCH NOM MNCH NOM

HERE YOU GO!

HAMBURGER STEAK, GRILLED EEL, AND FRIED CHICKEN!

....!!

NO WAY! IT'S HIDEOUS!

YEAH!! MY BOO BOUGHT THIS BAG FOR ME!!

REALLY, HEBIKO?!

GUY'S GOT NO FASHION SENSE! WA HA HA!

DON'T WORRY.

UM, IGURO SENSEI?

HM?

I'M FINE.

KANROJI ISN'T LIKE THAT.

DO THEY HAVE TO BE...

...SO LOUD?

HE EVEN SAID HE SPENT ALL DAY PICKING IT OUT!!

EW! CREEPY!!

TITTER TITTER GIGGLE GIGGLE GUFFAW

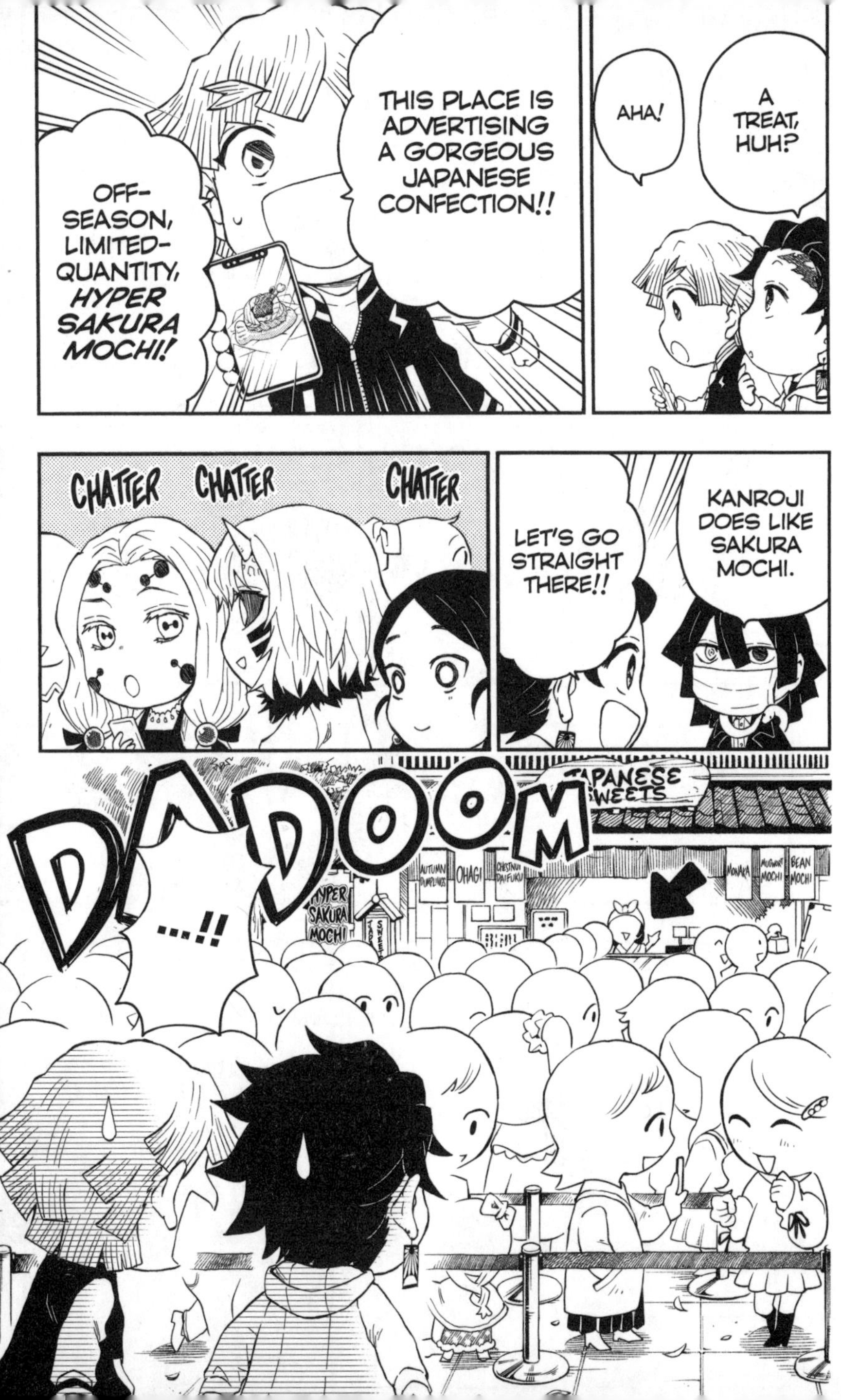
A TREAT, HUH?
AHA!
THIS PLACE IS ADVERTISING A GORGEOUS JAPANESE CONFECTION!!
OFF-SEASON, LIMITED-QUANTITY, HYPER SAKURA MOCHI!
KANROJI DOES LIKE SAKURA MOCHI.
LET'S GO STRAIGHT THERE!!
CHATTER
CHATTER
CHATTER
JAPANESE SWEETS
BEAN MOCHI
MUGWORT MOCHI
MONAKA
CHESTNUT DAIFUKU
OHAGI
AUTUMN DUMPLINGS
HYPER SAKURA MOCHI
DADOOM
...!!

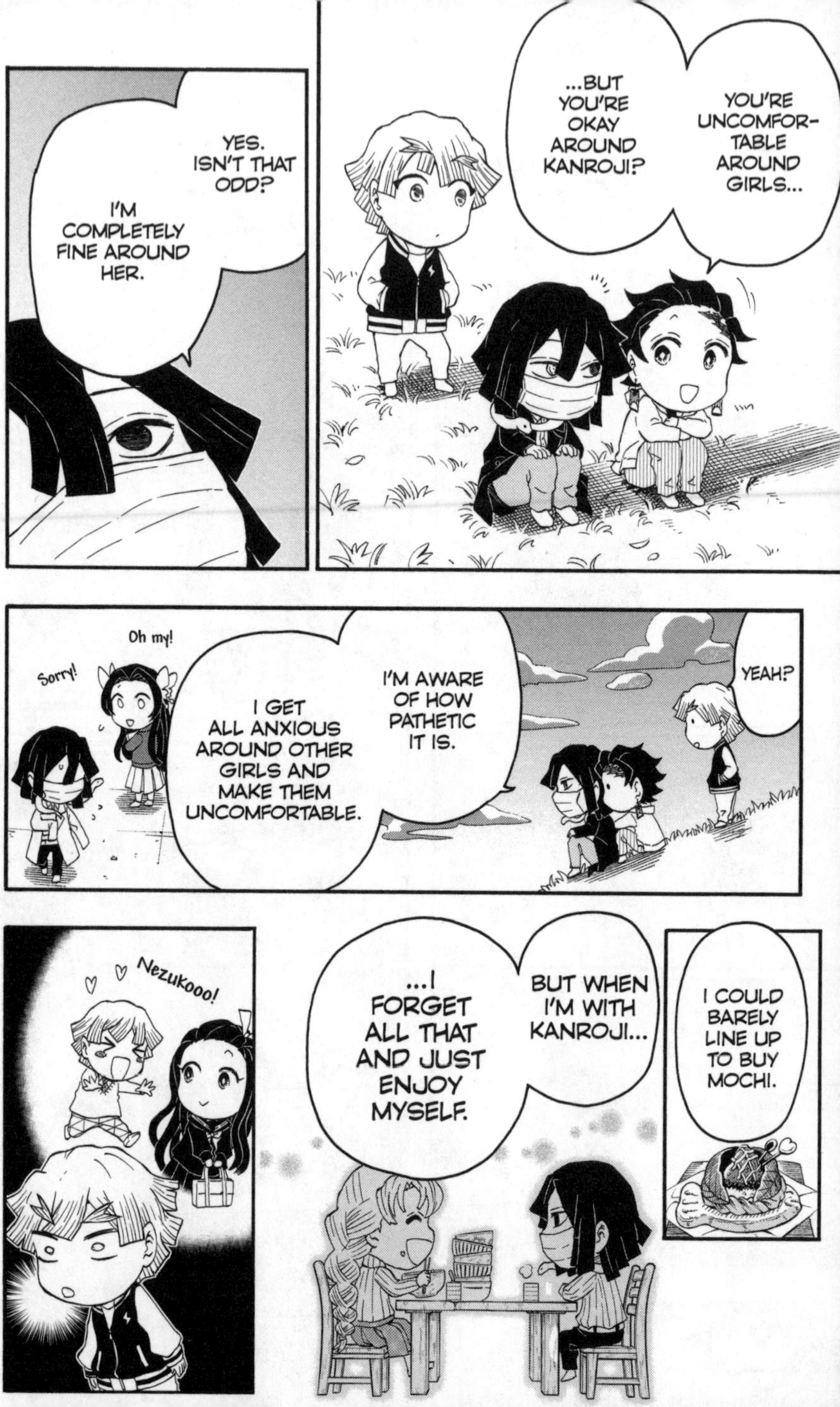
YOU'RE UNCOMFORTABLE AROUND GIRLS...
...BUT YOU'RE OKAY AROUND KANROJI?
YES. ISN'T THAT ODD?
I'M COMPLETELY FINE AROUND HER.
YEAH?
I'M AWARE OF HOW PATHETIC IT IS.
I GET ALL ANXIOUS AROUND OTHER GIRLS AND MAKE THEM UNCOMFORTABLE.
Oh my!
Sorry!
I COULD BARELY LINE UP TO BUY MOCHI.
BUT WHEN I'M WITH KANROJI...
...I FORGET ALL THAT AND JUST ENJOY MYSELF.
Nezukooo!

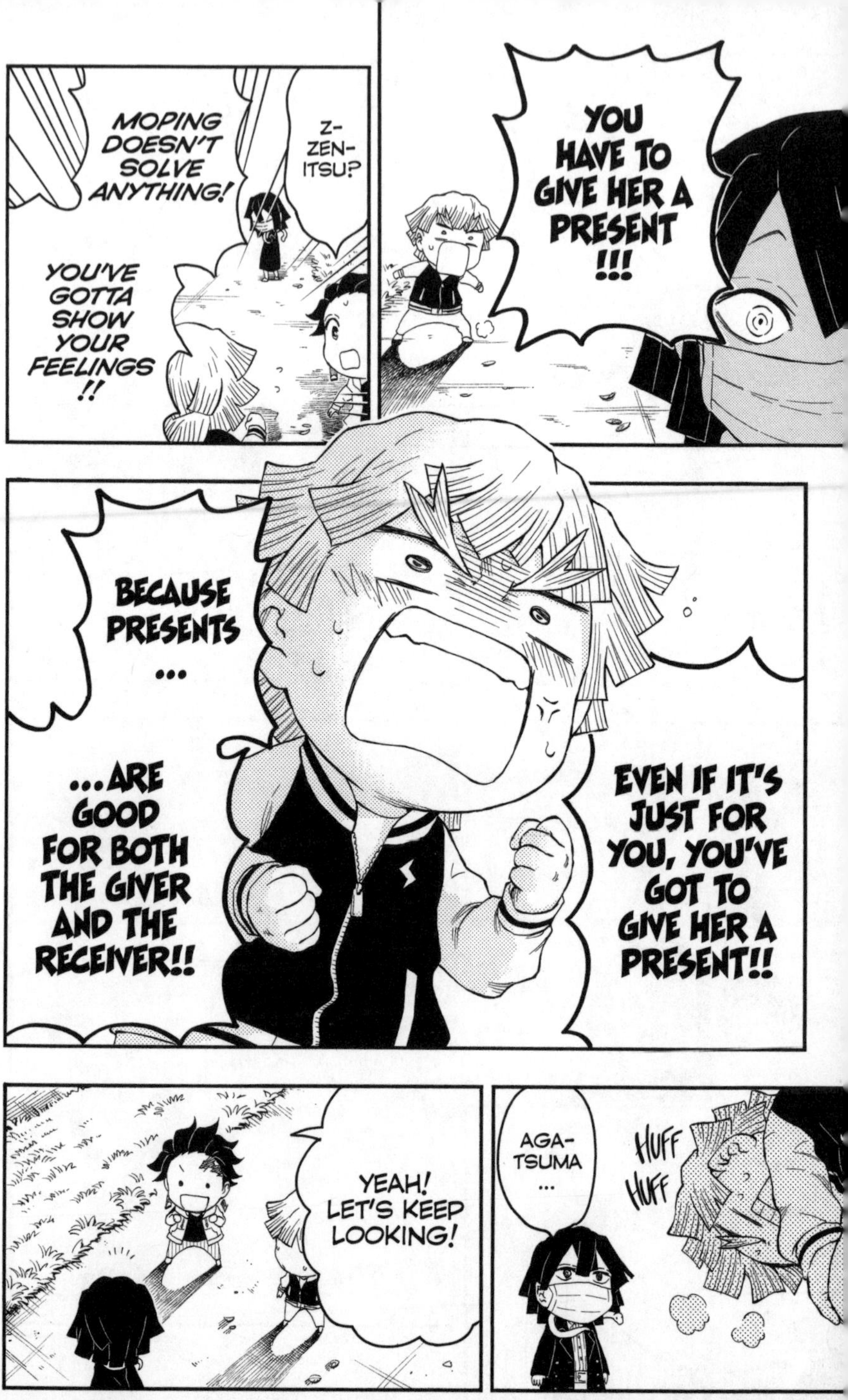
YOU HAVE TO GIVE HER A PRESENT!!!
Z-ZEN-ITSU?
MOPING DOESN'T SOLVE ANYTHING!
YOU'VE GOTTA SHOW YOUR FEELINGS!!
BECAUSE PRESENTS...
...ARE GOOD FOR BOTH THE GIVER AND THE RECEIVER!!
EVEN IF IT'S JUST FOR YOU, YOU'VE GOT TO GIVE HER A PRESENT!!
HUFF HUFF
AGA-TSUMA...
YEAH! LET'S KEEP LOOKING!

BY THE WAY...

...I BROUGHT SOMETHING FOR YOU.

RUSTL

OH?

I LOVE HAVING DINNER WITH YOU!!

OPEN IT UP.

I HAD NO IDEA!

A PRESENT?! WHAT A SURPRISE!!

OOH! WHAT CUTE SOCKS!

I HAD TO GO TO WORK ...

...SO I HAVE NO IDEA WHAT IT IS!

TEE HEE HEE!

B DMP B DMP

AND THEY'VE GOT—!

BIG HAND CAT IS AN ORIGINAL CHARACTER...

...THAT KANROJI DESIGNED AS AN ART STUDENT.

Lookie, Iguro!

I SEARCHED ONLINE FOR A SHOP...

...THAT WOULD EMBROIDER THEM BASED ON YOUR ILLUSTRATION.

I ALSO HAD THEM EMBROIDER...

...SOMETHING FOR ME.

I WANTED TO DO IT MYSELF, BUT IT WAS TOO DIFFICULT.

This place'll do it!!

Here, Sensei!!

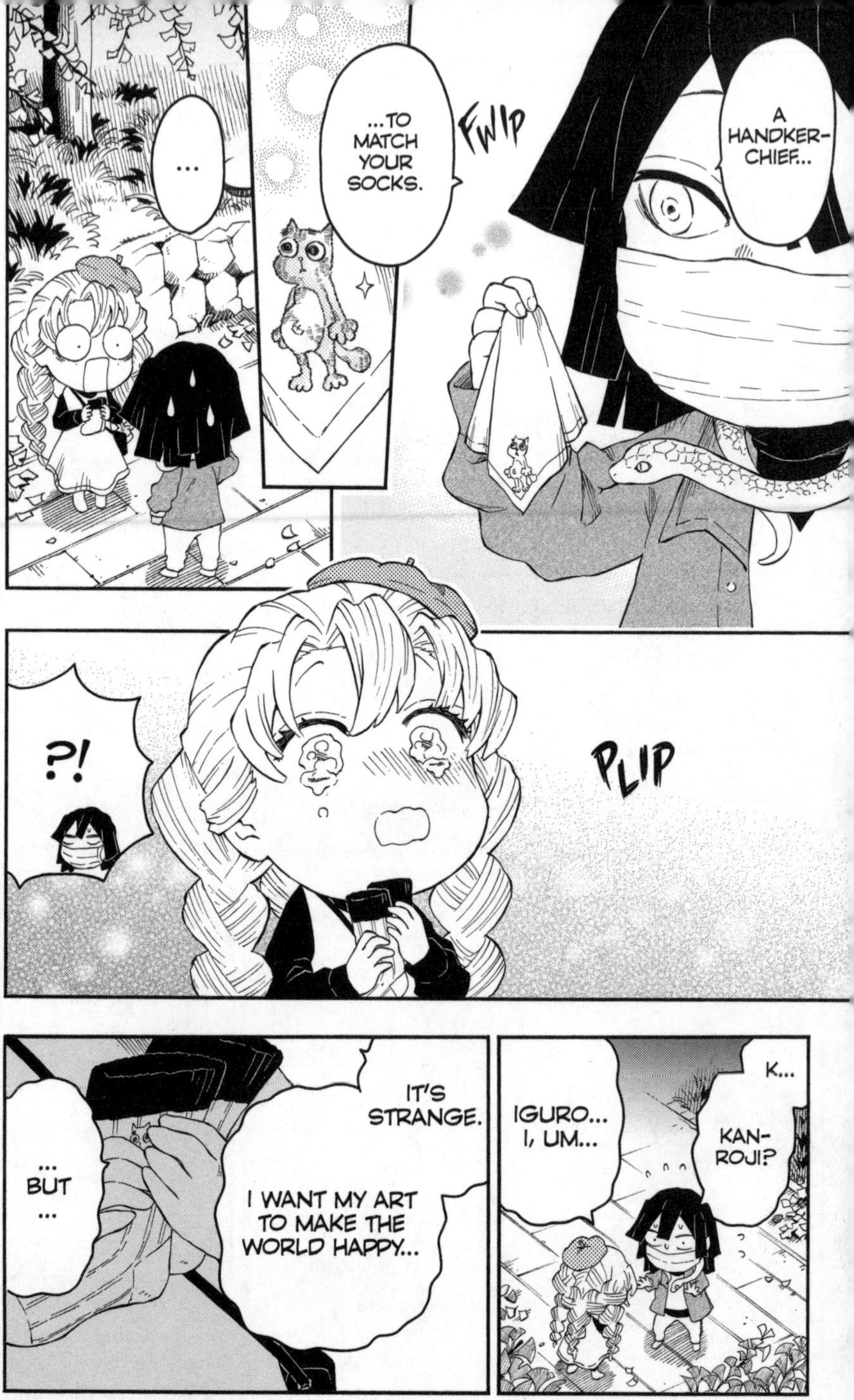
A HANDKER-CHIEF...
FWIP
...TO MATCH YOUR SOCKS.
...
PLIP
?!
K...
KAN-ROJI?
IGURO... I, UM...
IT'S STRANGE.
I WANT MY ART TO MAKE THE WORLD HAPPY...
... BUT ...

CHAPTER 10 DELETED SCENES
USELESS TEACHERS

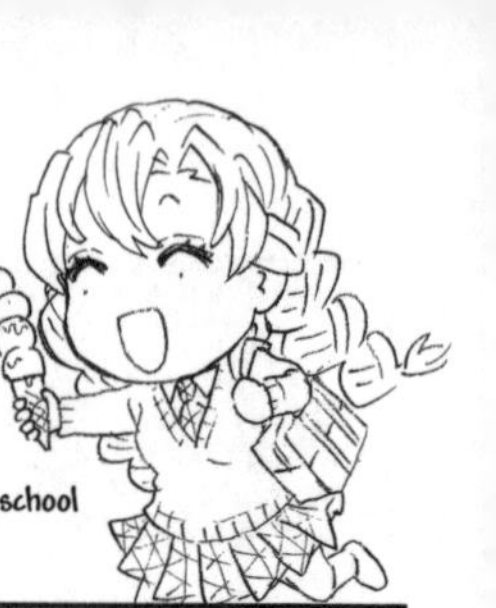

Kanroji in high school

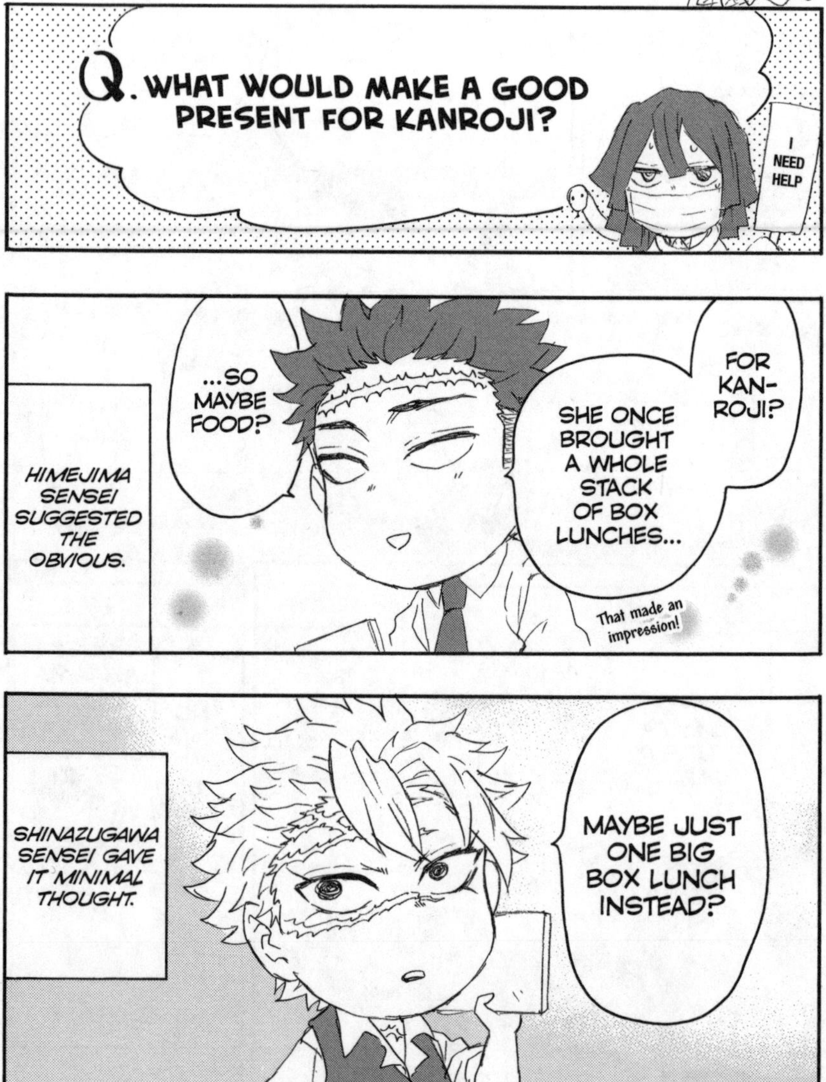
Q. WHAT WOULD MAKE A GOOD PRESENT FOR KANROJI?
I NEED HELP
FOR KAN-ROJI?
SHE ONCE BROUGHT A WHOLE STACK OF BOX LUNCHES...
That made an impression!
...SO MAYBE FOOD?
HIMEJIMA SENSEI SUGGESTED THE OBVIOUS.
MAYBE JUST ONE BIG BOX LUNCH INSTEAD?
SHINAZUGAWA SENSEI GAVE IT MINIMAL THOUGHT.

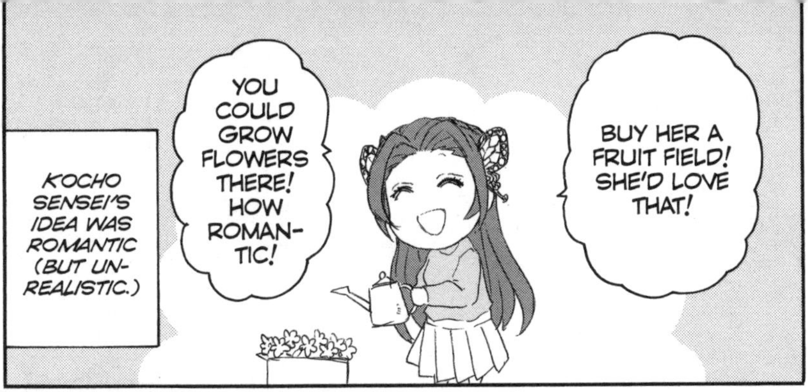
BUY HER A FRUIT FIELD! SHE'D LOVE THAT!
YOU COULD GROW FLOWERS THERE! HOW ROMAN-TIC!
KOCHO SENSEI'S IDEA WAS ROMANTIC (BUT UN-REALISTIC.)

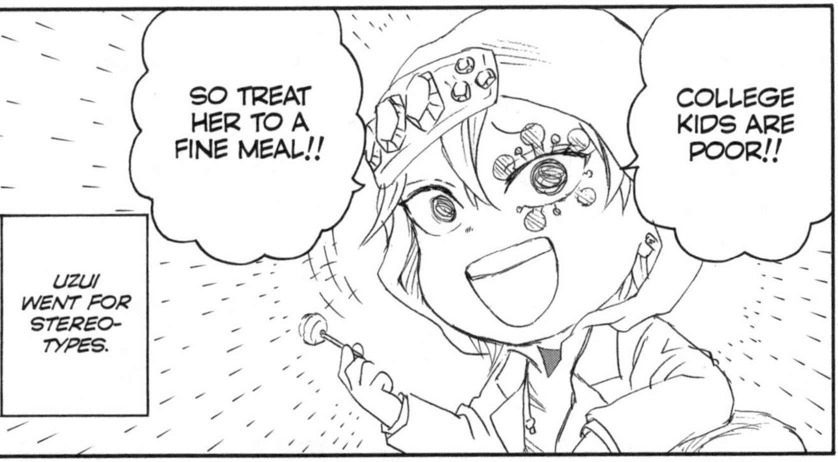
COLLEGE KIDS ARE POOR!!
SO TREAT HER TO A FINE MEAL!!
UZUI WENT FOR STEREO-TYPES.

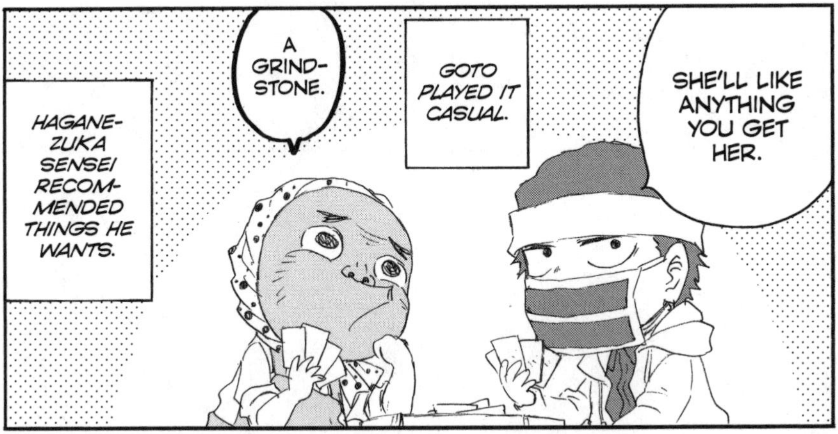
SHE'LL LIKE ANYTHING YOU GET HER.
GOTO PLAYED IT CASUAL.
A GRIND-STONE.
HAGANE-ZUKA SENSEI RECOM-MENDED THINGS HE WANTS.

KYOGAI SENSEI WAS THOUGHTFUL.

...SO STUFF HER WITH FOOD.

SHE CAN'T BUY FROM THE SCHOOL KIOSK ANYMORE...

DESPITE BEING HER FORMER TEACHER, RENGOKU WAS STILL RENGOKU.

HOW ABOUT A BAG OF RICE?!

HE DIDN'T BOTHER ASKING TOMIOKA SENSEI.

THAT EXPLAINS IT.

...

WHICH ONLY LEFT...

VOLUME 2 (END)

THIS IS TAMIO ENMU.

TANJIRO ALWAYS CATCHES HIM MISBEHAVING ON THE TRAIN.*

*SEE VOL. 1, CHAPTER 1.

HE'S A TRAIN GEEK WITH A CRIMINAL HABIT.

*EYES: LOWER ONE

BONUS CHAPTER: KUMOTORI STATION, 7:30 A.M.

...

TMP
TMP
TMP

FOMP

GWOOOOOIO

YOU MAKE ME SOUND LIKE A FLASHER!

WELL, AREN'T YOU?

YES, I AM.

HOW RUDE!

SO I CAN NAB YOU WHEN YOU MOON PEOPLE!

WHY DID YOU SIT NEXT TO ME?

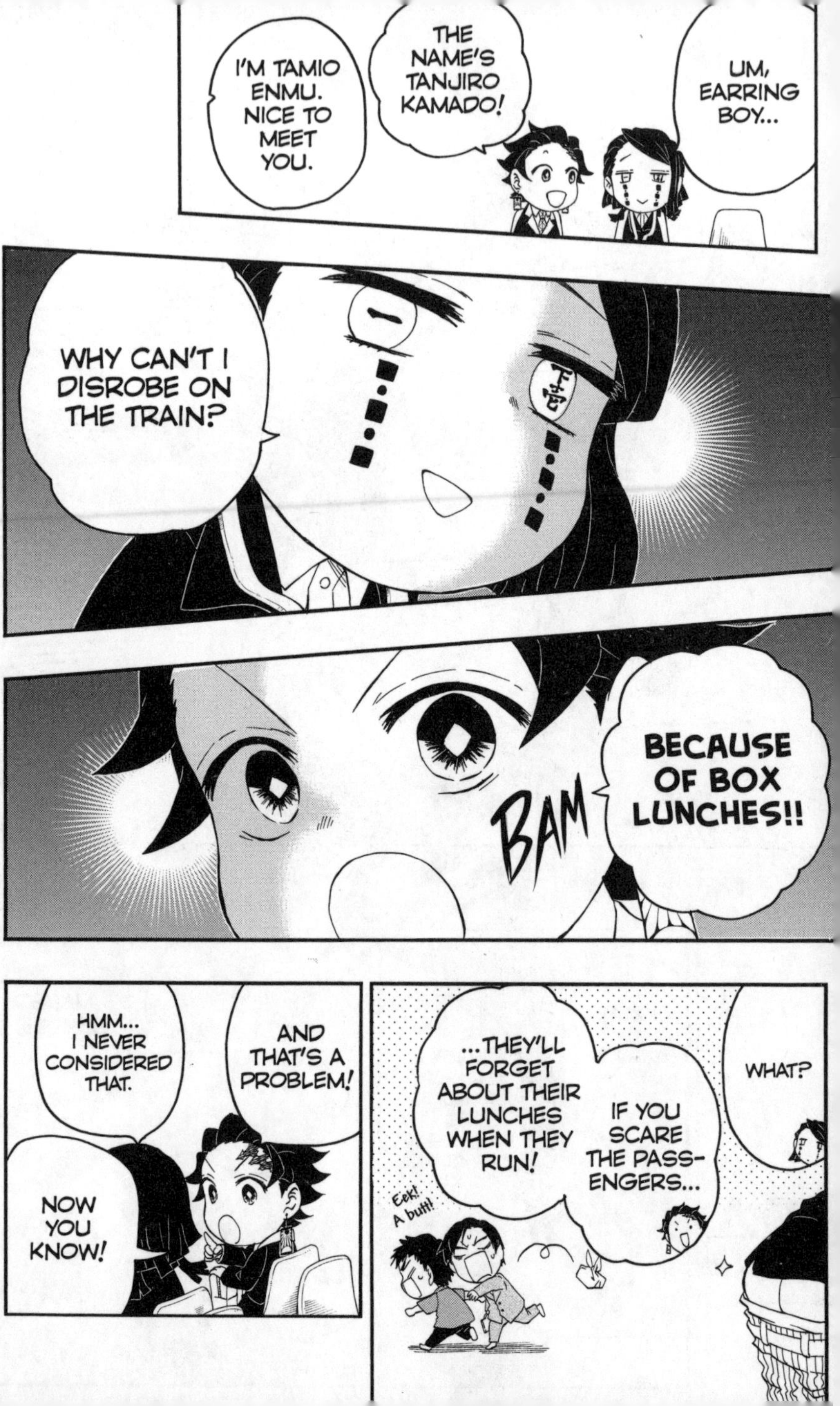
UM, EARRING BOY...
THE NAME'S TANJIRO KAMADO!
I'M TAMIO ENMU. NICE TO MEET YOU.
WHY CAN'T I DISROBE ON THE TRAIN?
BECAUSE OF BOX LUNCHES!!
BAM
WHAT?
IF YOU SCARE THE PASS-ENGERS...
...THEY'LL FORGET ABOUT THEIR LUNCHES WHEN THEY RUN!
Eek! A butt!
AND THAT'S A PROBLEM!
HMM... I NEVER CONSIDERED THAT.
NOW YOU KNOW!

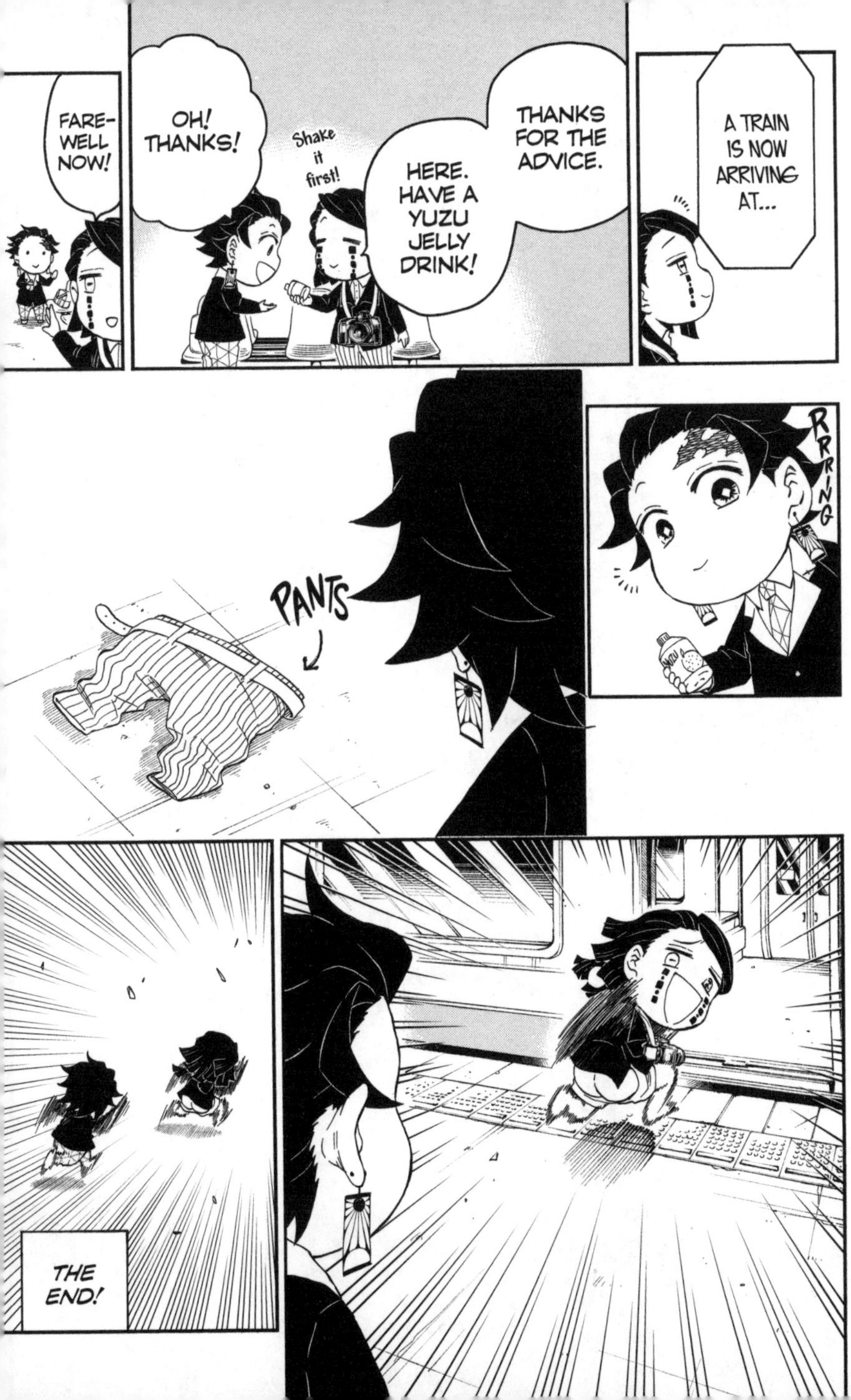
A TRAIN IS NOW ARRIVING AT...
THANKS FOR THE ADVICE.
HERE. HAVE A YUZU JELLY DRINK!
Shake it first!
OH! THANKS!
FARE-WELL NOW!
RRRING
YUZU
PANTS
THE END!

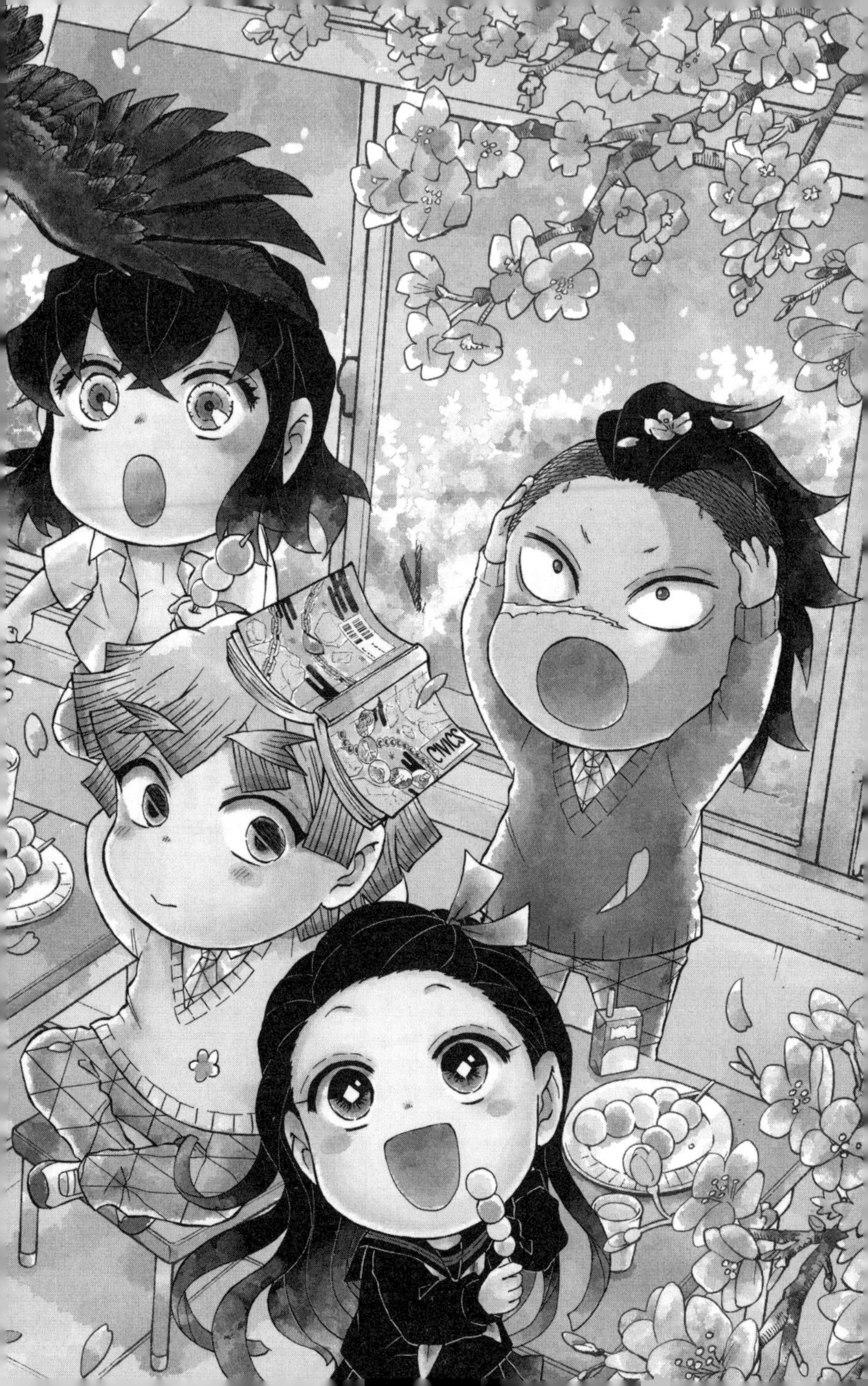
CIVICS

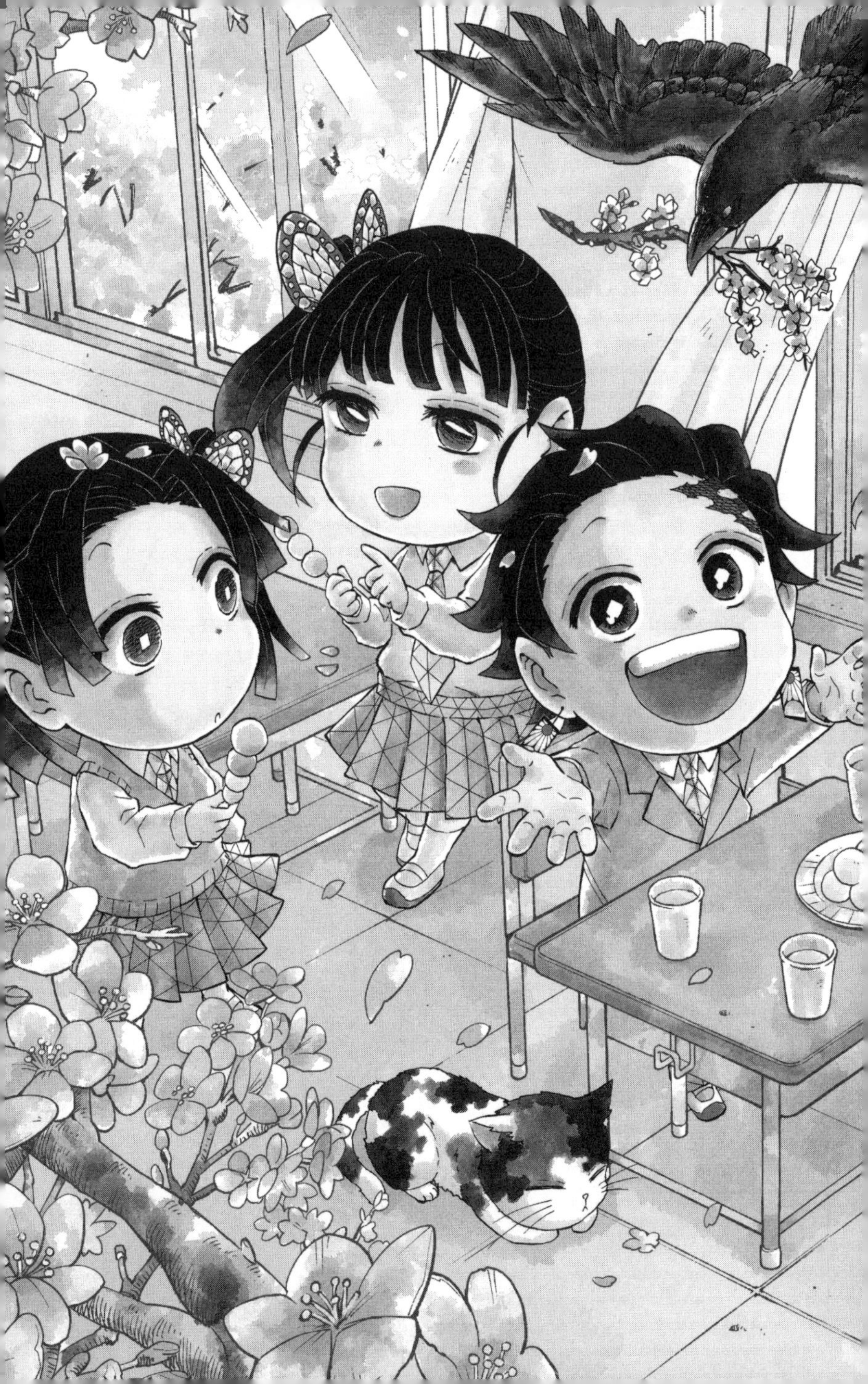

AFTERWORD

Welcome to volume 2! Thanks for reading! Just like with volume 1, this was only possible through the efforts of a lot of people, so thank you all very much. I'll be counting on you in the future too.

This volume goes on sale in July, and the story takes place from early summer to autumn, so I'm thrilled to see how the seasons have synced up. What a happy coincidence!

The serialized releases never match the actual season, so I drew the preceding two-page spread to match with the real world. Without any connection to the story, the sakura trees are in full bloom! I have to say, I like that illustration, but I was never satisfied with the color illustration of Makomo and the others for chapter 9, so I put them on the back cover of this volume.

I suspect volume 3 will take place from autumn to winter. Nothing is slated yet, though, so here's hoping it gets the green light!

STAFF

REGULARS
Nagashima
Kantaro Kumano
Keisuke Futta

HELPERS
Kojiro
Tachi Biwa

SPECIAL THANKS
Saikyo Jump editor: Toide-san
The *Demon Slayer: Kimetsu no Yaiba* original manga team
Graphic novel editor: Abe-san
Designers: Deguchi-san, Abe-san
Original creator: Koyoharu Gotouge
All the readers!

Natsuki Hokami

帆上夏希.

Good work! This is Gotouge! Volume 2 of *Kimetsu Academy* is on sale! Here's a big thanks to Hokami Sensei, the editors, assistants, and readers! The number of characters playing a role is ramping up, making these pages more boisterous than ever!

As the fun continues to take off, I hope you'll come along for the ride!!

FIRST-YEAR TEXTBOOK DESIGNS
FOR KIMETSU ACADEMY HIGH SCHOOL

For a while, I only had a rough idea for these,
but I asked my staff and they came up with proper designs.
The other grades basically look the same.

You're reading the wrong way!

In keeping with the original Japanese comic format, *Demon Slayer: Kimetsu Academy* reads from right to left, meaning that action, sound effects, and word-balloon order are completely reversed from English order.

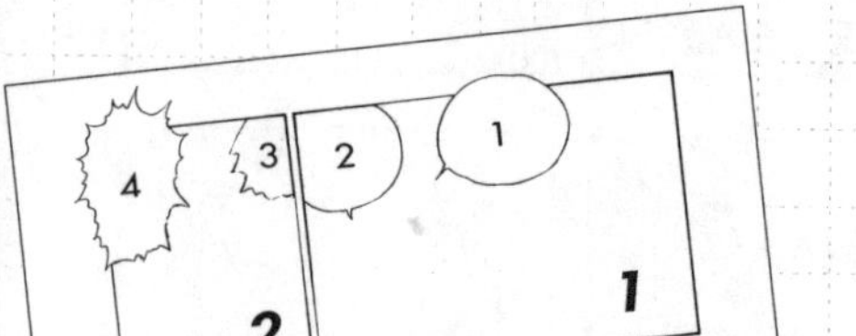
1
1
2
3
2
4
5
6
3
7
8
4
9
5
142

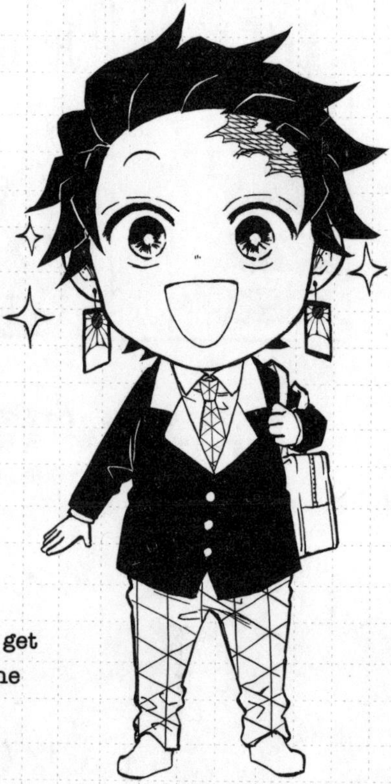

Check out the diagram shown here to get the hang of things, and then turn to the other side of the book to get started!